NATEF Correlated T

for

Automotive Brake Systems

Seventh Edition

James D. Halderman

rotors = pads

Drums = Shoes

PEARSON

Boston Columbus Indianapolis New York San Francisco
Amsterdam Cape Town Dubai London Madrid Milan Munich Paris Montreal Toronto
Delhi Mexico City São Paulo Sydney Hong Kong Seoul Singapore Taipei Tokyo

Editor-in-Chief: Andrew Gilfillan
Product Manager: Anthony Webster
Program Manager: Holly Shufeldt
Project Manager: Rex Davidson
Editorial Assistant: Nancy Kesterson
Team Lead Project Manager: Bryan Pirrmann
Team Lead Program Manager: Laura Weaver
Director of Marketing: David Gesell
Senior Product Marketing Manager: Darcy Betts

Field Marketing Manager: Thomas Hayward
Procurement Specialist: Deidra M. Skahill
Creative Director: Andrea Nix
Art Director: Diane Y. Ernsberger
Cover Designer: Cenveo
Full-Service Project Management: Abinaya Rajendran
Composition: Integra Software Services, Ltd.
Printer/Binder: RR Donnelley Harrisonburg

ISBN 10: 0-13-407242-1
ISBN 13: 978-0-13-407242-5

Contents

Chapter 1 – Service Information, Tools, and Safety

Safety Check (None Specified)   1

Vehicle Hoisting (None Specified)   2

Fire Extinguisher (None Specified)   3

Work Order (A5-A-1)   4

Vehicle Brake System Information (A5-A-3)   5

Base Brake Identification (A5-A-3)   6

VIN Code (A5-A-4)   7

Chapter 2 – Environmental and Hazardous Materials

Material Safety Data Sheet (None Specified)   8

Chapter 3 – Braking System Components and Performance Standards

Identify and Interpret Brake Concerns (A5-A-2)   9

Brake System Component Identification (None Specified)   10

Chapter 4 – Braking System Principles and Friction Materials

Brake System Principles (None Specified)   11

Brake Performance Identification (None Specified)   12

Chapter 5 – Brake Hydraulic Systems

Hydraulic Pressure Analysis (A5-B-1)   13

Brake Pedal Height (A5-B-2)   14

Master Cylinder Operation Testing (A5-B-3)   15

Bench Bleeding the Master Cylinder (A5-B-4)   16

Hydraulic System Fault Analysis (A5-B-5)   17

Chapter 6 – Hydraulic Valves and Switches

Metering Valve Inspection and Testing (A5-B-10)   18

Proportioning Valve Inspection and Testing (A5-B-10)   19

Pressure Differential Switch Inspection (A5-B-10)   20

Height-Sensing Proportioning Valves (A5-B-10)   21

Red Brake Warning Lamp Diagnosis (A5-B-11)   22

Brake Stop Light System (A5-F-5)   23

Chapter 7 – Brake Fluid and Lines

Brake Hose and Line Inspection (A5-B-6)   24

Brake Line and Hose Replacement (A5-B-7)   25

Brake Line Flaring (A5-B-8)   26

Brake Fluid (A5-B-9)   27

Brake Fluid Contamination Test (A5-B-13)   28

iv

Chapter 8 – Brake Bleeding Methods and Procedures

Manual Brake Bleeding (A5-B-12)   29
Pressure Brake Bleeding (A5-B-12)   30
Vacuum Brake Bleeding (A5-B-12)   31
Gravity Brake Bleeding (A5-B-12)   32
Surge Brake Bleeding (A5-B-12)   33
Brake Fluid Flush and Fill (A5-B-12)   34

Chapter 9 – Wheel Bearings and Service

Wheel Bearing Diagnosis (A5-F-1)   35
Wheel Bearing Service (A5-F-2)   36
Wheel Bearing and Race Replacement (A5-F-6)   37
Inspect and Replace Wheel Studs (A5-F-8)   38
Sealed Wheel Bearing Replacement (A5-F-7)   39

Chapter 10 – Drum Brakes

Drum Brake Identification (None Specified)   40

Chapter 11 – Drum Brake Diagnosis and Service

Drum Brake Problem Diagnosis (A5-C-1)   41
Drum Brake Inspection (A5-C-4)   42
Drum Brake Overhaul (A5-C-4)   43
Dual Servo Drum Brake (A5-C-4)   44
Leading/Trailing Drum Brake (A5-C-4)   45
Wheel Cylinder Inspection and Replacement (A5-C-5)   46
Pre-Adjustment of Brake Shoes (A5-C-6)   47
Install Wheel and Torque Lug Nuts (A5-A-4)   48

Chapter 12 – Disc Brakes

Disc Brake Identification (None Specified)   49

Chapter 13 – Disc Brake Diagnosis and Service

Disc Brake Problem Diagnosis (A5-D-1)   50
Front Disc Brake Inspection (A5-D-2)   51
Caliper Mounting and Slide (A5-D-3)   52
Remove and Inspect Disc Brake Pads (A5-D-4)   53
Disc Brake Caliper Overhaul (A5-D-5)   54
Disc Brake Caliper Assembly (A5-D-6)   55
Brake Pad Wear Indicator System (A5-D-11)   56
Disc Brake Pad Burnish/Break-In (A5-D-12)   57

Chapter 14 – Parking Brake Operation, Diagnosis, and Service

Rear Disc Parking Brake Adjustment (A5-D-10) 58

Parking Brake Adjustment (A5-F-3) 59

Parking Brake Operation (A5-F-4) 60

Parking Brake Indicator Light (A5-F-5) 61

Chapter 15 – Machining Brake Drums and Rotors

Brake Drum Measurement (A5-C-2) 62

Machining a Brake Drum (A5-C-3) 63

Brake Rotor Measurement (A5-D-6) 64

Remove and Replace a Disc Brake Rotor (A5-D-7) 65

On-the-Vehicle Lathe (A5-D-8) 66

Machining a Brake Rotor (A5-D-9) 67

Chapter 16 – Power Brake Unit Operation, Diagnosis, and Service

Vacuum Power Brake Booster Test (A5-E-1) 68

Vacuum Supply/Manifold or Auxiliary Pump (A5-E-2) 69

Vacuum-Type Power Booster Unit (A5-E-3) 70

Hydro-Boost Test (A5-E-4) 71

Master Cylinder Pushrod Length (A5-E-5) 72

Chapter 17 – ABS Components and Operation

Traction Control Identification (A5-G-9) 73

Chapter 18 – ABS Diagnosis and Service

ABS Component Inspection (A5-G-1) 74

ABS Component Identification (A5-G-1) 75

Diagnose ABS System Concerns (A5-G-4) 76

ABS Code Retrieval and Erase (A5-G-5) 77

ABS Set a Code/Retrieve a Code (A5-G-5) 78

Depressurization of High-Pressure ABS (A5-G-6) 79

Bleed ABS Hydraulic Circuits (A5-G-7) 80

Remove and Install ABS Components (None Specified) 81

ABS Wheel Speed Sensor Testing (A5-G-8) 82

Modified Vehicle ABS Problem Diagnosis (A5-G-9) 83

Chapter 19 – Electronic Stability Control System

Traction Control/Vehicle Stability Component Identification (A5-G-2) 84

Chapter 20 – Regenerative Braking Systems

Regenerative Braking System Identification (A5-G-3) 85

Appendix – Student Check Off Sheets

 86

Safety Check

Meets NATEF Task: None Specified

Name _____ Date _____ Time on Task _____

Make/Model _____ Year _____ Evaluation: 4 3 2 1

_____ **1.** Check the headlights (brights and dim).

_____ **2.** Check the taillights.

_____ **3.** Check the side marker lights.

_____ **4.** Check the license plate light.

_____ **5.** Check the brake lights.

_____ **6.** Check the turn signals.

_____ **7.** Check the back-up lights with the ignition switch "on" (engine "off") and the gear selector in reverse.

_____ **8.** Check the windshield wipers (all speeds) and wiper blades.

_____ **9.** Check the heater-defroster fan (all speeds).

_____ **10.** Check the condition of the tires (must have at least 2/32" of tread) and the tire pressure. Do not forget to check the spare tire!

_____ **11.** Check for looseness in the steering wheel (less than 2" of play).

_____ **12.** Check the 4-way emergency flashers.

_____ **13.** Check the horn.

_____ **14.** Listen for exhaust system leaks.

_____ **15.** Check the parking brake (maximum 8-10 "clicks" and should "hold" in drive).

Vehicle Hoisting

Meets NATEF Task: None Specified

Name _____ Date _____ Time on Task _____

Make/Model _____ Year _____ Evaluation: 4   3   2   1

Getting Ready to Hoist the Vehicle

_____ 1. Drive the vehicle into position to be hoisted (lifted) being certain to center the vehicle in the stall.

_____ 2. Pull the vehicle forward until the front tire rests on the tire pad (if equipped).

NOTE: Some long vehicles may have to be positioned forward of the pad and some short vehicles may have to be positioned behind the pad.

_____ 3. Place the gear selector into the park position (if the vehicle has an automatic transmission/transaxle) or in neutral (if the vehicle has a manual transmission/transaxle) and firmly apply the parking brake.

_____ 4. Position the arms and hoist pads under the frame or pinch weld areas of the body.

Hoisting the Vehicle

_____ 5. Slowly raise the vehicle about one foot (30 cm) off the ground and check the stability of the vehicle by attempting to move the vehicle on the lift. Reposition pads if needed.

NOTE: Best working conditions are at chest or elbow level.

_____ 6. Be sure the safety latches have engaged before working under the vehicle.

Lowering the Vehicle

_____ 7. To lower the vehicle, raise the hoist slightly, then release the safety latches.

_____ 8. Lower the vehicle using the proper operating and safety release levers.

CAUTION: Do not look away while lowering the vehicle. One side of the vehicle could become stuck or something (or someone) could get under the vehicle.

_____ 9. After lowering the hoist arms all the way to the floor, move the arms so that they will not be hit when the vehicle is driven out of the stall.

Fire Extinguisher

Meets NATEF Task: None Specified

Name _____ Date _____ Time on Task _____

Make/Model _____ Year _____ Evaluation: 4 3 2 1

_____ **1.** Describe the location of the fire extinguishers in your building or shop and note the last inspection dates.

Type of Extinguisher	Location	Inspection Date
_____	_____	_____
_____	_____	_____
_____	_____	_____
_____	_____	_____

_____ **2.** Do any of the fire extinguishers need to be charged?

_____ Yes (which ones) _____

_____ No

_____ **3.** Where can the fire extinguishers be recharged? List the name and telephone number of the company. _____

_____ **4.** What is the cost to recharge the fire extinguishers?

a. Water = _____

b. CO_2 = _____

c. Dry chemical = _____

Work Order

Meets NATEF Task: (A5-A-1) Complete work order to include customer information, vehicle identifying information, customer concern, service history, cause, and correction. (P-1)

Name _____ Date _____ Time on Task _____

Make/Model _____ Year _____ Evaluation: 4 3 2 1

Fill in the customer and vehicle information, plus the customer concerns and related service history.

UAS Automotive
1415 Any Street
City, State 99999

NATEF
ASE CERTIFIED PROGRAM

Customer Information   Name _____
Daytime _____   Address _____
Evening _____   City _____ State _____ Zip _____

Vehicle Information
Year _____   Model _____
Color _____   Mileage _____
VIN _____

Materials
_____
_____
_____
_____
_____
_____
_____
_____
_____
_____
_____
_____
_____
_____
_____
_____
_____
_____

Customer Concern _____
_____
_____
_____
_____
_____

Related Service History _____
_____
_____

Labor Performed _____
_____
_____

Root Cause of Problem _____
_____
_____

Customer Authorization

X _____

Totals

Materials _____
Labor _____
Misc. _____
Sub Total _____
Tax _____
TOTAL _____

Vehicle Brake System Information

Meets NATEF Task: (A5-A-3) Research vehicle service information. (P-1)

Name _____ Date _____ Time on Task _____

Make/Model _____ Year _____ Evaluation: 4 3 2 1

Consult vehicle manufacturer's service information to determine the following:

_____ **1.** Brake related technical service bulletins (TSBs):

      A. Topic _____ Bulletin Number _____

      Problem/Correction: _____

      B. Topic _____ Bulletin Number _____

      Problem/Correction: _____

_____ **2.** Front brake service information:

      A. Minimum thickness of front disc brake pads:

      _____

      B. Minimum thickness of front disc brake rotor:

      _____

_____ **3.** Rear brake service information:

      A. Minimum thickness of rear friction material:

      _____

      B. Maximum allowable drum or minimum allowable rear disc brake rotor

      thickness: _____

_____ **4.** ABS/hydraulic service information:

      A. Brand and type of ABS: _____

      B. Bleeding procedure: _____, _____, _____, _____

      C. Wheel speed sensor resistance/gap: Front = _____ Rear = _____

_____ **5.** Research the vehicle's service history and record all brake system-related previous

      service or repairs.

      _____

      _____

Base Brake Identification

Meets NATEF Task: (A5-A-3) Research applicable vehicle and service information. (P-1)

Name _____ **Date** _____ **Time on Task** _____

Make/Model _____ **Year** _____ **Evaluation:** 4 3 2 1

_____ **1.** The vehicle being inspected is equipped with what type of base brakes?

      _____ Four-wheel drum brakes (old vehicles)

      _____ Four-wheel disc brakes

      _____ Front disc brakes/rear drum brakes

      _____ Other (describe) _____

_____ **2.** Is the vehicle equipped with an antilock braking system?

      _____ Yes _____ No

      If yes, describe the type of system _____

_____ **3.** Consult the vehicle manufacturer's service information and determine the specified brake fluid:

      _____ DOT 3

      _____ DOT 4

      _____ DOT 5.1

      _____ DOT 5.0

      _____ Other (specify) _____

_____ **4.** Check the condition of the brake fluid.

      _____ Clear (like new)

      _____ Amber

      _____ Dark amber

      _____ Black

      _____ Other (describe)

VIN Code

Meets NATEF Task: (A5-A-4) Locate and interpret vehicle identification numbers. (P-1)

Name _____ **Date** _____ **Time on Task** _____

Make/Model _____ **Year** _____ **Evaluation:** 4   3   2   1

VIN Number _____

- The first number or letter designates the **country of origin** = _____

1 = United States	6 = Australia	L = China	V = France
2 = Canada	8 = Argentina	R = Taiwan	W = Germany
3 = Mexico	9 = Brazil	S = England	X = Russia
4 = United States	J = Japan	T = Czechoslovakia	Y = Sweden
5 = United States	K = Korea	U = Romania	Z = Italy

- The model of the vehicle is commonly the fourth or fifth character. **Model?** _____

- The eighth character is often the engine code. (Some engines cannot be determined by the VIN number.) **Engine code:** _____

- The tenth character represents the year on all vehicles. See the following chart.

VIN Year Chart (The pattern repeats every 30 years.)   **Year?** _____

A = 1980/2010	J = 1988/2018	T = 1996/2026	4 = 2004/2034
B = 1981/2011	K = 1989/2019	V = 1997/2027	5 = 2005/2035
C = 1982/2012	L = 1990/2020	W = 1998/2028	6 = 2006/2036
D = 1983/2013	M = 1991/2021	X = 1999/2029	7 = 2007/2037
E = 1984/2014	N = 1992/2022	Y = 2000/2030	8 = 2008/2038
F = 1985/2015	P = 1993/2023	1 = 2001/2031	9 = 2009/2039
G = 1986/2016	R = 1994/2024	2 = 2002/2032	
H = 1987/2017	S = 1995/2025	3 = 2003/2033	

Material Safety Data Sheet (MSDS)

Meets NATEF Task: None Specified

Name _____ Date _____ Time on Task _____

Make/Model _____ Year _____ Evaluation: 4 3 2 1

_____ **1.** Locate the MSDS sheets and describe their location _____

_____

_____ **2.** Select three commonly used chemicals or solvents. Record the following information from the MSDS:

• **Product name** _____

        chemical name(s) _____

        Does the chemical contain "chlor" or "fluor" which may indicate

        hazardous materials? **Yes** _____ **No** _____

        flash point = _____ (hopefully above 140° F)

        pH _____ (7 = neutral, higher than 7 = caustic (base),

        lower than 7 = acid)

• **Product name** _____

        chemical name(s) _____

        Does the chemical contain "chlor" or "fluor" which may indicate hazardous

        materials? **Yes** _____ **No** _____

        flash point = _____ (hopefully above 140° F)

        pH _____ (7 = neutral, higher than 7 = caustic (base), lower than 7 = acid)

• **Product name** _____

        chemical name(s) _____

        Does the chemical contain "chlor" or "fluor" which may indicate hazardous

        materials? **Yes** _____ **No** _____

        flash point = _____ (hopefully above 140° F)

        pH _____ (7 = neutral, higher than 7 = caustic (base), lower than 7 = acid)

Identify and Interpret Brake Concerns

Meets NATEF Task: (A5-A-2) Identify and interpret brake system concern and determine necessary action. (P-1)

Name Luke Schneider **Date** _____ **Time on Task** _____

Make/Model _____ **Year** _____ **Evaluation:** 4 3 2 1

_____ **1.** Verify the customer's concern regarding brake system performance and identify areas of concern (check all that apply).

        _____ Red brake warning light on
        _____ Amber ABS warning light on
        _____ Noise during braking
        _____ Noise while driving
        _____ Pulling during braking
        _____ Hard brake pedal
        _____ Low brake pedal
        _____ Spongy brake pedal
        _____ Pulsating brake pedal
        _____ Steering wheel vibration
        _____ Other (describe) _____

_____ **2.** Perform a thorough visual inspection and note any possible problems.

        _____ Tires (all the same brand, size, inflation, and condition)
            _____ **OK** _____ **NOT OK** **Describe** _____

        _____ Brake fluid (check all that apply)
            _____ **OK** _____ **Dirty** _____ **Low**

        _____ Front disc brakes
            _____ **OK** _____ **NOT OK** **Describe** _____

        _____ Rear brakes
            _____ **OK** _____ **NOT OK** **Describe** _____

        _____ Hydraulic lines, parts, and fittings
            _____ **OK** _____ **NOT OK** **Describe** _____

_____ **3.** Based on the symptoms and the inspection, what service and/or parts will be needed to restore like-new braking system performance?

_____

_____

Brake System Component Identification

Meets NATEF Task: None Specified

Name _____ **Date** _____ **Time on Task** _____

Make/Model _____ **Year** _____ **Evaluation:** 4 3 2 1

_____ **1.** Front disc brake design type (check all that apply):

    ___ A. Single piston caliper
    ___ B. Piston caliper
    ___ C. Four or six piston caliper
    ___ D. Fixed-type caliper design
    ___ E. Floating- or sliding-type caliper design

_____ **2.** Front rotor:

    ___ A. Vented
    ___ B. Solid

_____ **3.** Rear brakes (check all that apply):

    ___ A. Drum brakes
    ___ B. Disc brakes with integral parking brake
    ___ C. Disc brake with auxiliary parking drum brake
    ___ D. Other (describe) _____

_____ **4.** Type of parking brake application:

    ___ Hand operated
    ___ Foot operated
    ___ Electric

_____ **5.** Type of parking brakes (check which):

    ___ Drum brake
    ___ Part of rear disc brake
    ___ Separate drum brake along with rear disc brake
    ___ Other (describe) _____

Brake System Principles

Meets NATEF Task: None Specified

Name _____ Date _____ Time on Task _____

Make/Model _____ Year _____ Evaluation: 4 3 2 1

The energy required to slow and/or stop a vehicle depends on two major factors:

- Weight of the vehicle
- Speed of the Vehicle

_____ **1.** Check service information and determine the weight of the vehicle.

Weight = _____

_____ **2.** Add the number of possible passengers (one for each location equipped with seat belts times 150 pounds each):

Number of passengers = _____ × 150 pounds = _____

_____ **3.** Add possible luggage or cargo (see tire pressure decal) weight:

Luggage or cargo = _____

_____ **4.** Total vehicle weight = _____

_____ **5.** Using the formula, determine the kinetic energy at the following speeds:

$$\frac{weight \times speed^2}{29.9} = kinetic\ energy$$

30 mph = _____

60 mph = _____

Brake Performance Identification

Meets NATEF Task: None Specified

Name _____ Date _____ Time on Task _____

Make/Model _____ Year _____ Evaluation: 4 3 2 1

_____ **1.** Check the front brakes for the following (check all that apply):

      ___ A. Vented rotors
      ___ B. Air scoop to front brakes
      ___ C. Grooved (slotted) rotors
      ___ D. Cross drilled rotors

_____ **2.** Antilock braking system (ABS) (check all that apply):

      ___ A. Not equipped with ABS
      ___ B. Rear wheel antilock
      ___ C. Three-channel antilock
      ___ D. Four-channel antilock
      ___ E. Remote-type antilock
      ___ F. Unknown

_____ **3.** Check all that can turn on the red brake warning lamp:

      ___ A. Parking brake applied
      ___ B. Low brake fluid level in the master cylinder reservoir
      ___ C. Unequal brake pressure in the system

Hydraulic Pressure Analysis

Meet NATEF Task: (A5-B-1) Diagnose pressure concerns in the brake system using hydraulic principles. (P-1)

Name _____ Date _____ Time on Task _____

Make/Model _____ Year _____ Evaluation: 4 3 2 1

_____ **1.** Remove the disc brake calipers and install a force gauge between the caliper piston and the caliper housing.

_____ **2.** Depress the brake pedal and observe the force readings.

   Left side = _____ pounds   Right side = _____ pounds

   The readings should be the same.   **OK** _____   **NOT OK** _____

_____ **3.** List possible causes that could prevent the force reading to be different from one side to the other.

   A. _____

   B. _____

   C. _____

_____ **4.** Based on the test results, what is the necessary action?

   _____

   _____

Brake Pedal Height

Meet NATEF Task: (A5-B-2) Measure brake pedal height; determine necessary action. (P-1)

Name _____ **Date** _____ **Time on Task** _____

Make/Model _____ **Year** _____ **Evaluation:** 4 3 2 1

_____ **1.** State the vehicle manufacturer's specified brake height testing procedure:

_____

_____

_____

_____ **2.** Measure the brake pedal height from the bottom of the steering wheel or floor to the brake pedal.

_____ = inch (cm)

_____ **3.** Depress the brake pedal until the brakes are applied and measure the brake pedal height.

_____ = inch (cm)

_____ **4.** Subtract the second reading from the first reading. This is the brake pedal travel.

_____ = brake pedal travel (should be a maximum of 2.0 to 2.5 in.)

_____ **5.** List three items that could cause a greater than normal brake pedal travel.

A. _____

B. _____

C. _____

_____ **6.** Based on the test results, what is the necessary action: _____

_____

Master Cylinder Operation Testing

Meet NATEF Task: (A5-B-3) Check master cylinder for external and internal leaks and proper operation. (P-1)

Name _____ Date _____ Time on Task _____

Make/Model _____ Year _____ Evaluation: 4 3 2 1

_____ **1.** Check visually for signs of external brake fluid
leaks.

        _____ **OK** _____ **NOT OK**

        Describe location _____

_____ **2.** Check for internal leakage by observing the
level of brake fluid in the front compared
to the rear.

        A. Is the level higher in the front than the rear? _____ **Yes** _____ **No**

        B. Is the brake pedal lower than normal? _____ **Yes** _____ **No**

If yes to both A and B above, then the master cylinder is leaking internally and must
be replaced.

_____ **3.** Have an assistant depress the brake pedal while watching the brake fluid in the master
cylinder reservoir. The brake fluid should be seen to move as the brake pedal is being
depressed if the sealing caps are OK and positioned correctly.

        Movement observed? _____ **Yes** _____ **No**

If brake fluid does not move and there is a breaking system problem, the master
cylinder or linkage adjustment is faulty.

_____ **4.** Based on the test results, what is the necessary action? _____

_____

Bench Bleeding the Master Cylinder

Meet NATEF Task: (A5-B-4) Bench bleed master cylinder. (P-1)

Name _____ Date _____ Time on Task _____

Make/Model _____ Year _____ Evaluation: 4 3 2 1

Before a replacement master cylinder is installed in a vehicle, most vehicle manufacturers recommend that the master cylinder be bled.

_____ 1. Clamp the ears of the master cylinder in a suitable vise.

> **CAUTION:** Do not clamp the body of the master cylinder or bore distortion can occur.

_____ 2. Install tubes into the outlets of the master cylinder and direct the tubes near the top of the open reservoir.

_____ 3. Fill the master cylinder reservoir with clean DOT 3 brake fluid from a sealed container.

_____ 4. Using a blunt tool, such as a rounded dowel rod or a Phillips screwdriver, slowly stroke the master cylinder.

_____ 5. Continue stroking the master cylinder until a solid stream of brake fluid is observed flowing out of the tubes and into the reservoir.

_____ 6. Remove the bleeding tubes and unclamp the master cylinder. The master cylinder can now be installed on the vehicle where additional bleeding at the outlet fitting may be necessary.

Hydraulic System Fault Analysis

Meet NATEF Task: (A5-B-5) Diagnose braking concerns caused by hydraulic malfunctions.
(P-3)

Name _____ Date _____ Time on Task _____

Make/Model _____ Year _____ Evaluation: 4 3 2 1

Poor stopping or dragging brakes or pulling can be caused by hydraulic system failure or faults.

_____ **1.** Check master cylinder for proper brake fluid level and condition.

_____ **2.** Verify proper operation of the base brakes.
       _____ OK
       _____ Pulls to the left during braking (see Step 3).
       _____ Pulls to the right during braking (see Step 3).
       _____ Brakes do not release fully (see Step 4).
       _____ Poor stopping (see Step 5).
       _____ Other brake system concerns (describe)
       _____

_____ **3.** Pulling can be caused by a stuck caliper piston on the side *opposite* the direction of the pull.

       If there is a pull to the right during braking, check the left side caliper.
           OK _____   **NOT OK** _____

       If there is a pull to the left during braking, check the right side caliper.
           OK _____   **NOT OK** _____

_____ **4.** Brakes that do not fully release can be caused by a fault with the flexible brake hose and/or a stuck caliper piston

       Visually check the flexible brake hose.   **OK** _____   **NOT OK** _____

       Check that the caliper piston can be moved into the caliper bore easily.
           OK _____   **NOT OK** _____

_____ **5.** Poor stopping can be caused by a stuck caliper or wheel cylinder piston. Check that all hydraulic pistons are free.

       LF = **OK** _____   **NOT OK** _____   LR = **OK** _____   **NOT OK** _____
       RF = **OK** _____   **NOT OK** _____   RR= **OK** _____   **NOT OK** _____

18

Metering Valve Inspection and Testing

Meet NATEF Task: (A5-B-10) Inspect, test, and/or replace metering (hold-off) proportioning (balance), pressure differential, and combination valves. (P-3)

Name _____ Date _____ Time on Task _____

Make/Model _____ Year _____ Evaluation: 4 3 2 1

A defective metering valve can leak brake fluid and/or cause the front brakes to apply before the rear brakes. This is most commonly noticed on slippery surfaces such as on snow or ice or on rain-slick roads. If the front brakes lock up during these conditions, the front wheels cannot be steered. Inspect the metering for these two conditions:

_____ 1. Check the vehicle manufacturer's service information for the recommended metering valve testing procedure:

_____

_____ 2. Leakage - Look at the bottom on the metering valve for brake fluid leakage. (Ignore slight dampness.) Replace the metering valve assembly if leaking.

_____ 3. As the pressure builds to the front brakes, the metering valve stem should move. If it does not, replace the valve.

_____ 4. More accurate testing of the metering valve can be accomplished using pressure gauges. Install two gauges, one in the pressure line coming from the master cylinder and the other in the outlet line leading to the front brakes.

_____ 5. Depress the brake pedal. Both gauges should read the same until about 3-30 psi (20 to 200 kPa) when the metering valve shuts thereby delaying the operation of the front brakes.

_____ 6. The master cylinder outlet gauge should show an increase in pressure as the brake pedal is depressed further.

_____ 7. Once 75 to 300 psi is reached, the gauge showing pressure to the front brakes should match the pressure from the master cylinder. If the pressures do not match these ranges, the metering valve assembly should be replaced.

NOTE: Neither the metering valve nor the proportioning valve can cause a pull to one side if defective. The metering valve controls *both* front brakes, and the proportioning valve controls *both* rear brakes. A defective master cylinder cannot cause a pull either. Therefore, if a vehicle pulls to one side during a stop, look for problems in the individual wheel brakes, hoses or suspension.

19

Proportioning Valve Inspection and Testing

Meet NATEF Task: (A5-B-10) Inspect, test, and/or replace metering (hold-off) proportioning (balance), pressure differential, and combination valves. (P-3)

Name _____ Date _____ Time on Task _____

Make/Model _____ Year _____ Evaluation: 4 3 2 1

A defective proportioning valve usually allows rear brake pressure to increase too rapidly, causing the rear wheels to lock up during hard braking. If the proportioning valve is height sensing, verify proper vehicle ride (trim) height and adjustment of the operating lever.

_____ 1. Check service information for the specified method and test procedures to follow to test a proportioning valve.

_____ 2. Describe the location of the proportioning valve(s) and describe their condition:

_____

_____

_____ 3. Based on the inspection and testing, does the proportioning valve need to be replaced? Explain why or why not?

_____

_____

20

Pressure Differential Switch Inspection

Meet NATEF Task: (A5-B-10) Inspect, test, and/or replace metering (hold-off) proportioning (balance), pressure differential, and combination valves. (P-3)

Name _____ Date _____ Time on Task _____

Make/Model _____ Year _____ Evaluation: 4 3 2 1

_____ 1. A pressure-differential switch is used on all vehicles built after 1967 with dual master cylinders to warn the driver of a loss of pressure in one of the two separate systems by lighting the dashboard red brake warning indicator lamp.

_____ 2. The brake lines from both the front and the rear sections of the master cylinder are sent
to this switch which lights the brake warning indicator lamp in the event of a "difference in pressure" between the two sections.

_____ 3. A failure in one part of the brake system does not result in a failure of the entire hydraulic system. After the hydraulic system has been repaired and bled, moderate pressure on the brake pedal will center the piston in the switch and turn off the warning lamp.

_____ 4. If the lamp remains on, it may be necessary to:

    A. Apply light pressure to the brake pedal.
    B. Momentarily open the bleeder valve on the side that did not have the failure.

    This procedure should center the pressure differential switch valve in those vehicles not equipped with self-centering springs.

_____ 5. State the vehicle manufacturer's recommended inspection, testing, and replacement procedures:

_____

_____

_____

21

Height-Sensing Proportioning Valve

Meet NATEF Task: (A5-B-10) Inspect, test, and/or replace metering (hold-off) proportioning (balance), pressure differential, and combination valves. (P-3)

Name _____ Date _____ Time on Task _____

Make/Model _____ Year _____ Evaluation: 4 3 2 1

REAR
BRAKE TUBE

HEIGHT-SENSING
PROPORTIONING VALVE

OPERATING LEVER

BRACKET

BRAKE
TUBE

RETAINING
NUT

REAR BRAKE HOSE

_____ **1.** Describe the location of the height-sensing proportioning valve.

_____

_____

_____

_____ **2.** Visually check for leakage at the valve or damage to the linkage between the valve and the rear suspension.

   OK _____ **NOT OK** _____ Describe fault: _____

_____ **3.** List the steps specified by the service information regarding how the valves or linkage should be adjusted:

_____

_____

_____

22

Red Brake Warning Lamp Diagnosis

Meets NATEF Task: (A5-B-11) Inspect, test and/or replace components of brake warning light system. (P-2)

Name _____ Date _____ Time on Task _____

Make/Model _____ Year _____ Evaluation: 4 3 2 1

_____ 1. Does the vehicle use a brake fluid level sensor?

     ___ Yes ___ No

     (If yes, describe the location: _____.)

_____ 2. Does the vehicle use a pressure differential switch?

     ___ Yes ___ No

     (If yes, describe the location: _____.)

_____ 3. With the ignition key on, engine off (KOEO), apply the parking brake. Did the red brake warning lamp light?

     ___ Yes ___ No

     (If no, why not? _____)

_____ 4. Unplug the wiring connector from the brake fluid level sensor or pressure differential switch. With the key on, engine off (KOEO), did the red brake warning lamp light?

     ___ Yes ___ No   (It should not have come on.)

_____ 5. State the vehicle manufacturer's recommended inspection, testing, and replacement procedures:

     _____

     _____

     _____

     _____

23

Brake Stop Light Switch

Meets NATEF Task: (A5-F-5) Check operation of brake stop light system and determine necessary action. (P-1)

Name _____ Date _____ Time on Task _____

Make/Model _____ Year _____ Evaluation: 4 3 2 1

_____ 1. Check the service information for the specified testing procedures to determine the proper operation and adjustment of the brake stop light switch. _____

_____

_____

_____ 2. Check for the proper operation of the brake (stop) lights including the center high-mounted stop light (CHMSL).

OK ____ **NOT OK** ____

If not OK, determine the necessary action needed to restore proper operation.

_____

_____

_____ 3. Describe the location of the brake switch _____

_____ 4. Describe how to adjust the brake switch (if adjustable) _____

_____

_____ 5. List the trade number of the brake light bulbs, including the center high-mounted stop light.

Rear brake light trade number = _____

Center high-mounted stop light trade number = _____

_____ 6. Based on the test results, what is the necessary action? _____

_____

_____

24

Brake Hose and Line Inspection

Meet NATEF Task: (A5-B-6) Inspect brake lines and flexible hose for faults and determine necessary action. (P-1)

Name _____ **Date** _____ **Time on Task** _____

Make/Model _____ **Year** _____ **Evaluation:** 4 3 2 1

_____ 1. Hoist the vehicle safely.

_____ 2. Remove all four wheels.

_____ 3. Carefully inspect the flexible brake hoses on the left front, right front, and rear (one or two flexible hoses) for the following:

       _____ Leaks **OK** ___ **NOT OK** ___ Which hose(s)? _____

       _____ Kinks **OK** ___ **NOT OK** ___ Which hose(s)? _____

       _____ Cracks **OK** ___ **NOT OK** ___ Which hose(s)? _____

       _____ Bulges or wear **OK** ___ **NOT OK** ___ Which hose(s)? _____

_____ 4. Carefully inspect the steel brake lines from the master cylinder to the junction with the flexible brake lines and check for the following:

       _____ Leaks **OK** ___ **NOT OK** ___ Fault location? _____

       _____ Dents **OK** ___ **NOT OK** ___ Fault location? _____

       _____ Loose fittings or supports **OK** ___ **NOT OK** ___

       Fault location? _____

_____ 5. Based on the inspection, what is the necessary action? _____

_____

_____

25

Brake Line and Hose Replacement

Meet NATEF Task: (A5-B-7) Replace brake lines, hoses, fittings, and supports.
(P-2)

Name _____ Date _____ Time on Task _____

Make/Model _____ Year _____ Evaluation: 4 3 2 1

_____ **1.** Check service information for the procedure to follow when replacing brake line, hoses, fittings, and supports. Describe specified instructions:

_____

_____

_____ **2.** Check all that apply:

_____ Replaced both front flexible brake hoses

_____ Replaced rear flexible brake hose

_____ a. One?

_____ b. Two?

_____ Replaced steel brake line (describe location): _____

_____

_____

_____ a. What length? _____

_____ b. What diameter? _____

_____ c. What type of flare?

_____ Double flare?

_____ ISO (bubble) flare?

_____ **3.** What method was used to bleed the air from the brake hydraulic system?

_____

_____

_____

_____

_____

26

Brake Line Flaring

Meet NATEF Task: (A5-B-8) Fabricate brake lines using proper material and flaring procedures (double flare and ISO types). (P-2)

Name _____ Date _____ Time on Task _____

Make/Model _____ Year _____ Evaluation: 4 3 2 1

_____ **1.** Consult the vehicle manufacturer's service information and select the specified diameter of steel brake line. Which size outside diameter (O.D.) is needed for the application?

       _____ 3/16" (4.8 mm)

       _____ 1/4" (6.4 mm)

       _____ 5/16" (7.9 mm)

A

B

FIRST STEP   **FINISHED DOUBLE FLARE**

_____ **2.** Using a tubing bender, bend the sample line with a right angle (90°) bend.

      Instructor's OK _____

_____ **3.** Using the proper tool, perform a double flare on one end of the brake line.

      Instructor's OK _____

_____ **4.** Using the proper tool, perform an ISO flare on the other end of the brake line.

      Instructor's OK _____

27

Brake Fluid

Meet NATEF Task: (A5-B-9) Select, handle, store, and fill brake fluids to proper level. (P-1)

Name _____ Date _____ Time on Task _____

Make/Model _____ Year _____ Evaluation: 4 3 2 1

_____ 1. Consult the vehicle manufacturer's service information and determine the specified type of brake fluid.

　　　_____ DOT 3　　_____ DOT 4　　_____ Other (specify) _____

_____ 2. All brake fluid should be stored in a sealed container. Specify what type and size container of container is being used.

　　　_____ Metal (preferred because air containing moisture cannot penetrate metal)

　　　_____ Plastic (makes shelf life shorter because air containing moisture can penetrate most plastic)

　　　_____ Size (number of ounces or ml) _____

_____ 3. Brake fluid can remove paint so protective covers should be used whenever handling brake fluid. Check all that should be done when handling brake fluid.

　　　_____ Use fender covers

　　　_____ Wear protective gloves

_____ 4. Fill brake fluid to the "MAX" line on the master cylinder reservoir.

CAUTION: If the brake fluid level is too high, the brakes may self-apply when the normal operation of the wheel brakes warms the brake fluid, which expands in volume. If the brake fluid is unable to expand in the master cylinder reservoir, the pressure increases and the brakes can be applied even though the driver did not depress the brake pedal.

28

Brake Fluid Contamination Test

Meets NATEF Task: (A5-B-13) Test brake fluid for contamination. (P-1)

Name _____ Date _____ Time on Task _____

Make/Model _____ Year _____ Evaluation: 4 3 2 1

_____ 1. Check service information for the procedure to follow when checking brake fluid for contamination. Describe specified instructions:

_____

_____

_____ 2. What method was used to test brake fluid for contamination? (check all that apply)

_____ Test strips

_____ Electronic boiling point tester

_____ Placed brake fluid in a Styrofoam cup and checked for a ring indicating mineral oil was in the brake fluid

_____ Allowed to sit in a container and checked for separation

_____ Other (describe) _____

_____

_____ 3. Describe the results of the brake fluid contamination test. _____

_____

_____

29

Manual Brake Bleeding

Meets NATEF Task: (A5-B-12) Bleed and/or flush brake system. (P-1)

Name _____ Date _____ Time on Task _____

Make/Model _____ Year _____ Evaluation: 4   3   2   1

_____ **1.** Check the service information for the specified brake bleeding procedure for the vehicle being serviced.

_____ **2.** Fill the master cylinder reservoir with clean brake fluid from a sealed container.

_____ **3.** Hoist the vehicle safely.

_____ **4.** Open the right rear bleeder valve and have an assistant slowly depress the brake pedal to bleed the wheel cylinder/caliper. Close the bleeder valve and have the assistant slowly release force on the brake pedal. Wait 15 seconds and repeat the process until a solid stream of brake fluid is observed.

_____ **5.** Repeat the bleeding procedures for the left-rear, right-front, and then the left-front wheel brakes.

_____ **6.** After all four wheel brakes have been bled, lower the vehicle and fill the master cylinder to the full mark.

CAUTION: Check the master cylinder reservoir frequently and refill as necessary with clean brake fluid. Do not overfill a master cylinder reservoir.

_____ **7.** Test drive the vehicle checking for proper brake operation before returning the vehicle to the customer.

30

Pressure Brake Bleeding

Meets NATEF Task: (A5-B-12) Bleed and/or flush brake system. (P-1)

Name _____ Date _____ Time on Task _____

Make/Model _____ Year _____ Evaluation: 4 3 2 1

_____ **1.** Check the service information for the specified brake bleeding procedure for the vehicle being serviced.

_____ **2.** Fill the master cylinder reservoir with clean brake fluid from a sealed container.

_____ **3.** Hoist the vehicle safely.

_____ **4.** Open the right rear bleeder valve and use a pressure bleeder attached to the master cylinder using the correct adapter(s) to bleed the wheel cylinder/caliper until a solid stream of brake fluid is observed.

_____ **5.** Repeat the bleeding procedures for the left-rear, right-front, and then the left-front wheel brakes.

_____ **6.** After all four wheel brakes have been bled, lower the vehicle and fill the master cylinder to the full mark.

> **CAUTION:** Check the master cylinder reservoir frequently and refill as necessary with clean brake fluid. Do not overfill a master cylinder reservoir.

_____ **7.** Test drive the vehicle checking for proper brake operation before returning the vehicle to the customer.

31

Vacuum Brake Bleeding

Meets NATEF Task: (A5-B-12) Bleed and/or flush the brake system. (P-1)

Name _____ Date _____ Time on Task _____

Make/Model _____ Year _____ Evaluation: 4 3 2 1

_____ **1.** Check the service information for the specified brake bleeding procedure for the vehicle being serviced.

_____ **2.** Fill the master cylinder reservoir with clean brake fluid from a sealed container.

_____ **3.** Hoist the vehicle safely.

_____ **4.** Open the right rear bleeder valve and use a hand-operated or air-operated vacuum bleeder to bleed the wheel cylinder/caliper until a solid stream of brake fluid is observed.

_____ **5.** Repeat the bleeding procedures for the left-rear, right-front, and then the left-front wheel brakes.

_____ **6.** After all four wheel brakes have been bled, lower the vehicle and fill the master cylinder to the full mark.

> **CAUTION:** Check the master cylinder reservoir frequently and refill as necessary with clean brake fluid. Do not overfill a master cylinder reservoir.

_____ **7.** Test drive the vehicle checking for proper brake operation before returning the vehicle to the customer.

32

Gravity Brake Bleeding

Meets NATEF Task: (A5-B-12) Bleed and/or flush the brake system. (P-1)

Name _____ Date _____ Time on Task _____

Make/Model _____ Year _____ Evaluation: 4 3 2 1

_____ 1. Check the service information for the specified brake bleeding procedure for the vehicle being serviced.

_____ 2. Fill the master cylinder reservoir with clean brake fluid from a sealed container.

_____ 3. Hoist the vehicle safely.

_____ 4. Open the right rear bleeder valve and wait until about a drip-per-second of brake fluid is observed coming out of the bleeder valve and close the bleeder valve.

_____ 5. Repeat the bleeding procedures for the left-rear, right-front, and then the left-front wheel brakes.

_____ 6. After all four wheel brakes have been bled, lower the vehicle and fill the master cylinder to the full mark.

> **CAUTION:** Check the master cylinder reservoir frequently and refill as necessary with clean brake fluid. Do not overfill a master cylinder reservoir.

_____ 7. Test drive the vehicle checking for proper brake operation before returning the vehicle to the customer.

33

Surge Brake Bleeding

Meets NATEF Task: (A5-B-12) Bleed and/or flush the brake system. (P-1)

Name _____ Date _____ Time on Task _____

Make/Model _____ Year _____ Evaluation: 4 3 2 1

_____ 1. Check the service information for the specified brake bleeding procedure for the vehicle being serviced.

_____

_____

_____

_____ 2. Slip the plastic hose over the bleeder screw of the wheel cylinder or caliper to be bled and submerge the end of the tube in the jar of brake fluid.

_____ 3. Open the bleeder screw approximately one-half turn.

_____ 4. With the bleeder screw *open*, have your assistant rapidly pump the brake pedal several times. Air bubbles should come out with the brake fluid.

_____ 5. While your assistant holds the brake pedal to the floor, close the bleeder screw.

_____ 6. Repeat steps 2 through 4 at each bleeder screw in the recommended order.

_____ 7. Re-bleed the system using one of the four other methods described above.

34

Brake Fluid Flush and Fill

Meets NATEF Task: (A5-B-12) Bleed and/or flush brake system. (P-1)

Name _____ Date _____ Time on Task _____

Make/Model _____ Year _____ Evaluation: 4 3 2 1

Many vehicle manufacturers recommend the replacement of brake fluid every 2 or 3 years (24,000 - 36,000 miles or 38,000 - 58,000 km).

_____ 1. Check the service information for the specified brake bleeding procedure for the vehicle being serviced.

_____

_____

_____ 2. Use a turkey baster or similar tool to remove most of the old brake fluid from the master cylinder reservoir.

_____ 3. Refill the master cylinder with new brake fluid from a sealed container.

_____ 4. Hoist the vehicle safely.

_____ 5. Bleed the brake fluid from the right rear wheel brake until clean brake fluid is observed.

_____ 6. Repeat the bleeding process for the left rear, right front, then the left front wheel brakes.

> **NOTE:** Check the level of the brake fluid often and refill as necessary. Do not allow the master cylinder reservoir to become empty.

_____ 7. After all the wheel brakes have been bled with clean brake fluid, lower the vehicle and test drive checking for proper operation of the brakes before returning the vehicle to the customer.

35

Wheel Bearing Diagnosis

Meets NATEF Task: (A5-F-1) Determine wheel bearing noises, wheel shimmy, and vibration concerns; determine necessary action. (P-3)

Name _____ Date _____ Time on Task _____

Make/Model _____ Year _____ Evaluation: 4 3 2 1

Worn or defective wheel bearings can cause a variety of concerns including:

Noise – usually a growl or rumble that changes tone with vehicle speed.

Wheel Shimmy – Can occur if the bearings are loose or excessively worn.

Vibration – Can occur if the bearings are loose or excessively worn.

_____ 1. Check service information for the recommended test procedures to follow to diagnose possible wheel bearing noise.

_____

_____

_____ 2. Drive the vehicle and check for abnormal noise that could be caused by a defective wheel bearing.

OK _____   NOT OK _____

HINT: A defective wheel bearing often sounds like a noisy winter tire but does not change tone when the vehicle is being driven over various road surfaces.

_____ 3. Hoist the vehicle safely and check for excessive wheel bearing play and/or noise.

OK _____   NOT OK _____

Describe the faults and location: _____

_____ 4. Based on the diagnosis, what is the necessary action? _____

_____

36

Wheel Bearing Service

Meets NATEF Task: (A5-F-2) Remove, clean, inspect, repack, and install wheel bearings and replace seals; install hub and adjust bearings. (P-1)

Name _____ Date _____ Time on Task _____

Make/Model _____ Year _____ Evaluation: 4 3 2 1

_____ 1. Remove the wheel cover and the hub dust cap (grease cap).

_____ 2. Remove and discard the cotter key.

_____ 3. Remove the spindle nut, washer and outer bearing.

_____ 4. Remove inner and outer bearing and grease seal.

_____ 5. Thoroughly clean the bearing in solvent and denatured alcohol or brake cleaner and blow it dry with compressed air.

_____ 6. Closely inspect the bearing for wear or damage.

_____ 7. Show the instructor the cleaned bearing.

Instructor's OK _____

_____ 8. Repack the bearing with the correct type of wheel bearing grease.

_____ 9. Install a new grease seal using a seal installing tool.

_____ 10. Correctly adjust the bearing preload:

  _____ Install the spindle nut and while rotating the tire assembly, tighten (snug only, 12 to 30 lb.-ft.) with a wrench to "seat" the bearing correctly in the race.
  _____ While still rotating the tire assembly, loosen the nut approximately 1/2 turn and then *hand tighten only*.
  _____ Install a new cotter key (the common size is 1/8" diameter and 1.5 inches long).
  _____ Bend the ends of the cotter key up and around the nut to prevent interference with the dust cap.

_____ 11. Install the hub dust cap (grease cap) and wheel cover.

37

Wheel Bearing and Race Replacement

Meets NATEF Task: (A5-F-6) Replace wheel bearing and race. (P-2)

Name _____ Date _____ Time on Task _____

Make/Model _____ Year _____ Evaluation: 4 3 2 1

_____ **1.** Remove the wheel cover and the hub
dust cap (grease cap).

_____ **2.** Remove and discard the cotter key.

_____ **3.** Remove the spindle nut, washer and outer bearing.

_____ **4.** Remove inner and outer bearing and grease seal.

_____ **5.** Remove the bearing race using the specified tool.

_____ **6.** Show the instructor the removed race.

     Instructor's OK _____

_____ **7.** Install new race using the correct bearing race installation tool.

_____ **8.** Show the instructor the new race.

     Instructor's OK _____

_____ **9.** Install a new grease seal using a seal installing tool.

_____ **10.** Pack the new bearing with the correct type of wheel bearing grease.

_____ **11.** Correctly adjust the bearing preload:

    _____ Install the spindle nut and while rotating the tire assembly, tighten (snug
only, 12 to 30 lb.-ft.) with a wrench to "seat" the bearing correctly in the
race.
    _____ While still rotating the tire assembly, loosen the nut approximately 1/2 turn
and then *hand tighten only*.
    _____ Install a new cotter key (the common size is 1/8" diameter and 1.5 inches
long).
    _____ Bend the ends of the cotter key up and around the nut to prevent
interference with the dust cap.

_____ **12.** Install the hub dust cap (grease cap) and wheel cover.

38

Inspect and Replace Wheel Studs

Meets NATEF Task: (A5-F-8) Inspect and replace wheel studs. (P-1)

Name _____ Date _____ Time on Task _____

Make/Model _____ Year _____ Evaluation: 4 3 2 1

_____ **1.** Hoist the vehicle safely.

_____ **2.** Remove all four wheels.

_____ **3.** Carefully inspect the wheel studs for excessive rust or damage.

LF = OK _____ **NOT OK** _____ Describe fault _____

RF = OK _____ **NOT OK** _____ Describe fault _____

LR = OK _____ **NOT OK** _____ Describe fault _____

RR = OK _____ **NOT OK** _____ Describe fault _____

_____ **4.** Clean the threads using a stiff wire brush.

CAUTION: Many vehicle manufacturers specify that grease or oil should *not* be used on the threads of wheel studs. If a lubricant is used on the threads, the lug nuts could loosen during vehicle operation, which could cause a wheel to fall off resulting in a collision and possible personal injury.

_____ **5.** Worn or damaged studs should be replaced. Check the service information for the specified procedure for replacing wheel studs on the vehicle being serviced.

_____

_____ **6.** Which stud(s) were replaced? _____

39

Sealed Wheel Bearing Replacement

Meets NATEF Task: (A5-F-7) Remove and reinstall sealed wheel bearing assembly. (P-2)

Name _____ Date _____ Time on Task _____

Make/Model _____ Year _____ Evaluation: 4 3 2 1

_____ **1.** Check service information for the specified replacement procedure for the vehicle
being serviced. _____
_____

_____ **2.** Loosen (do not remove) the drive axle shaft nut.

_____ **3.** Hoist the vehicle safely to a good working height (about chest high).

_____ **4.** Remove the front wheel.

_____ **5.** Use a steel drift between the caliper and the rotor cooling vent hole to hold the rotor
from rotating.

_____ **6.** Remove the drive axle shaft hub nut.

_____ **7.** Remove the front disc brake caliper.

_____ **8.** Remove the rotor, the hub, and splash shield retaining bolts.

_____ **9.** Mark the location of the hub and make certain the hub is loose on the steering knuckle.

_____ **10.** Install the hub puller and remove the
bearing and hub assembly.

_____ **11.** Clean and lubricate hub bearing surface.

_____ **12.** Reinstall the hub and bearing using the
drive axle shaft nut. (Do not torque to the
final setting, just until the hub is seated.)

_____ **13.** Reinstall the rotor, caliper, and wheel.

_____ **14.** Lower the vehicle and tighten the drive axle shaft nut to the final specification.
Specification = _____ (usually about 200 lb.-ft.)

40

Drum Brake Identification

Meets NATEF Task: (None Specified)

Name _____ Date _____ Time on Task _____

Make/Model _____ Year _____ Evaluation: 4 3 2 1

_____ 1. Check service information and determine the following information regarding the drum brake design and features for the vehicle (check all that apply):

___ Dual servo
___ Leading trailing
___ Clip-on wheel cylinder
___ Bolted on wheel cylinder
___ Cast iron brake drum
___ Aluminum brake drum
___ Single U-spring design
___ Clip-type holddown
___ Coil-spring holddown
___ Cable-operated self adjust
___ Other (describe) _____
        _____
        _____

_____ 2. What is the brake drum diameter?

        _____

_____ 3. What is the minimum allowable lining thickness?

        _____

_____ 4. What is the maximum allowable brake drum diameter?

        _____

41

Drum Brake Problem Diagnosis

Meets NATEF Task: (A5-C-1) Diagnose poor stopping, noise, vibration, pulling, grabbing, dragging, or pedal pulsation concerns; determine necessary action. (P-1)

Name _____ Date _____ Time on Task _____

Make/Model _____ Year _____ Evaluation: 4   3   2   1

_____ **1.** Verify drum brake problem concerns.

         _____ Noise (describe) _____

         _____ Poor stopping

         _____ Pulling (toward which side?) _____

         _____ Grabbing (when?) _____

         _____ Dragging

         _____ Brake pedal pulsation

_____ **2.** Hoist the vehicle safely.

_____ **3.** Wet the brake drum or install a vacuum enclosure to provide protection against possible asbestos dust.

_____ **4.** Remove the brake drums.

_____ **5.** Describe the condition of the drum brake parts:

         _____ Brake drum _____

         _____ Lining _____

         _____ Springs _____

         _____ Self-adjuster _____

         _____ Backing plate _____

_____ **6.** Based on the diagnosis, what is the necessary action?

_____

_____

42

Drum Brake Inspection

Meets NATEF Task: (A5-C-4) Remove, clean, inspect drum brake parts; determine necessary action. (P-1)

Name _____ Date _____ Time on Task _____

Make/Model _____ Year _____ Evaluation: 4   3   2   1

_____ **1.** Hoist the vehicle safely to a good working height (about chest high).

_____ **2.** Remove the rear wheels.

_____ **3.** Remove the brake drums (they should pull straight off - if you have problems, see the instructor).

_____ **4.** Check the thickness of the lining remaining. (The brake lining should show equal thickness on both shoes and have a minimum thickness equal to the thickness of a nickel.)

  OK ____   **NOT OK** ____   **Describe any faults** _____

_____ **5.** Tap the brake drum with a steel hammer (it should ring like a bell)

  OK ____   **NOT OK** ____ **(discard)**

_____ **6.** Measure the inside diameter of the drum and compare to the specifications.

  Specifications = _____

  Actual: left = _____   right = _____

  OK ____   **NOT OK** ____

_____ **7.** Check for any brake fluid or rear axle fluid leakage.

  OK ____   **NOT OK** ____

_____ **8.** Based on this inspection, what is the necessary action?

  _____

  _____

43

Drum Brake Overhaul

Meets NATEF Task: (A5-C-4) Remove, clean, and inspect drum brake parts and reassemble.
(P-1)

Name _____ Date _____ Time on Task _____

Make/Model _____ Year _____ Evaluation: **4 3 2 1**

_____ **1.** Hoist the vehicle safely to a good working height (about chest high).

_____ **2.** Remove the rear wheels and the brake drums.

_____ **3.** Carefully inspect the brake drum.

- Hot (hard) spots   **OK**_____   **NOT OK**_____ (requires replacement)

- Tap with a hammer. The brake drum should ring like a bell if not cracked.

OK_____   **NOT OK**_____ (requires replacement)

_____ **4.** Measure the drum and replace or machine as necessary.

replace ـ____ machine ـ____

_____ **5.** Remove the old brake lining and hardware.

_____ **6.** Clean, inspect, and lubricate the backing plate.

_____ **7.** Inspect and replace the wheel cylinder as necessary.

_____ **8.** Clean and lubricate the star-wheel adjuster.

_____ **9.** Check or replace all hardware including the hold-down springs and return springs.

_____ **10.** Double check that the replacement brake shoes are the right size.

_____ **11.** Install the brake shoes, hardware, springs, and self adjuster.

_____ **12.** Adjust the brake shoes using a drum-shoe clearance gauge.

_____ **13.** Have the instructor check your work before installing the brake drum.

Instructor's OK _____

_____ **14.** Install the brake drum, wheel, and torque the lug nuts.

_____ **15.** Repeat on the other side of the vehicle.

_____ **16.** Lower the vehicle and check for proper brake operation.

44

Dual Servo Drum Brake

Meets NATEF Task: (A5-C-4) Remove, clean, and inspect drum brake parts and reassemble.
(P-1)

Name _____ Date _____ Time on Task _____

Make/Model _____ Year _____ Evaluation: 4 3 2 1

A dual servo (also called duo-servo) drum brake uses two brake shoes. The brake shoes attach to the wheel cylinder at the top and each other through an adjuster assembly at the bottom. The primary lining faces toward the front of the vehicle and use shorter linings than the rear (secondary) lining.

_____ 1. Hoist the vehicle safely to a good working height (about chest high).

_____ 2. Remove the rear wheels and brake drums.

_____ 3. Machine or replace the brake drum as needed.

_____ 4. Carefully clean the brake dust using an approved vacuum or liquid wash system.

_____ 5. Remove the return springs, hold-down springs, self adjuster, and brakes shoes.

_____ 6. Inspect the wheel cylinder and replace as necessary.

_____ 7. Clean and lubricate the backing plate.

_____ 8. Show the instructor the disassembled brake.

Instructor's OK _____

_____ 9. Reassemble the brakes.

_____ 10. Reinstall the brake drum and test the brakes for proper operation.

Brake spring tool

45

Leading/Trailing Drum Brake

Meets NATEF Task: (A5-C-4) Remove, clean, and inspect drum brake parts and reassemble.
(P-1)

Name _____ Date _____ Time on Task _____

Make/Model _____ Year _____ Evaluation: 4 3 2 1

A leading/trailing drum brake uses two equal length brake shoes that are anchored at the bottom and attached to the wheel cylinder at the top.

_____ 1. Hoist the vehicle safely to a good working height (about chest high).

_____ 2. Remove the rear wheels and brake drums.

_____ 3. Machine or replace the brake drum as needed.

_____ 4. Carefully clean the brake dust using an approved vacuum or liquid wash system.

_____ 5. Remove the return springs, hold-down springs, self adjuster, and brakes shoes.

_____ 6. Inspect the wheel cylinder and replace as necessary.

_____ 7. Clean and lubricate the backing plate.

_____ 8. Show the instructor the disassembled brake.

Instructor's OK _____

_____ 9. Reassemble the leading/ trailing brake.

_____ 10. Reinstall the brake drum and test the brakes for proper operation.

46

Wheel Cylinder Inspection and Replacement

Meets NATEF Task: (A5-C-5) Inspect and install wheel cylinders. (P-2)

Name _____ Date _____ Time on Task _____

Make/Model _____ Year _____ Evaluation: 4 3 2 1

_____ 1. Check the service information for the specified procedure for wheel cylinder replacement for the vehicle being serviced. _____

_____ 2. Hoist the vehicle safely and remove the rear wheels and brake drums.

_____ 3. Use a dull tool and lift the edge of the dust boots on the wheel cylinder.

        _____ Brake fluid dripped out (requires overhaul or replacement)
        _____ Dust boot is wet (normal, further inspection may be needed)
        _____ Dust boot is dry (normal, further inspection may be needed)

_____ 4. Remove the brake shoes to allow access to the wheel cylinders.

> **HINT:** Some service technicians apply the parking brake to force the brake shoe away from the wheel cylinder providing the clearance necessary to remove or replace the wheel cylinder without having to remove the brake shoe.

_____ 5. Remove the wheel cylinder from the backing plate and disassemble.

_____ 6. Clean the wheel cylinder with denatured alcohol or brake cleaner.

_____ 7. Clean and inspect the bore of the wheel cylinder.

        _____ Slightly pitted (can usually be restored to useful service by using crocus cloth and brake fluid)

> **NOTE:** Many vehicle manufacturers do not recommend using a cylinder hone because it would remove the special bearingized surface finish that is manufactured onto the inside surface of the wheel cylinder.

        _____ Heavily pitted (most manufacturers recommend replacement only).

_____ 8. After cleaning and inspection, do you overhaul or replace?

        _____ Overhaul using new seals and boots

        _____ Replacement with new wheel cylinders

_____ 9. Reinstall the wheel cylinders, brake linings, drums, and bleed the system.

_____ 10. Lower the vehicle and test the brakes for proper operation.

47

Pre-Adjustment of Brake Shoes

Meets NATEF Task: (A5-C-6) Pre-adjust brake shoes and parking brake; install brake drums or drum/hub assemblies and wheel bearings. (P-2)

Name _____ Date _____ Time on Task _____

Make/Model _____ Year _____ Evaluation: 4 3 2 1

Brake shoes should be pre-adjusted to close to the working clearance between the brake shoes and the brake drum before the brake drum is installed.

_____ **1.** Assemble the drum brake and verify that all parts are properly lubricated.

_____ **2.** Using a brake shoe clearance gauge, insert it into the drum and turn the lock knob to hold the setting.

_____ **3.** Install the brake shoe clearance gauge over the brake shoes and turn the adjuster until the lining contacts the gauge.

_____ **4.** Verify the pre-adjustment by installing the drum. It should slide over the brake shoes with little clearance.

OK _____ **NOT OK** _____

48

Install Wheel and Torque Lug Nuts

Meets NATEF Task: (A5-A-4) Install wheel and torque lug nuts and make final checks and adjustments. (P-1)

Name _____ Date _____ Time on Task _____

Make/Model _____ Year _____ Evaluation: 4 3 2 1

_____ **1.** Check service information and determine the vehicle manufacturer's specified lug nut torque specification.

_____ (usually between 80 and 100 lb-ft)

_____ **2.** Use a hand-operated wire brush on the wheel studs to ensure clean and dry threads and check for damage.

OK _____   **NOT OK** _____ Describe fault: _____

_____ **3.** Verify that the lug nuts are OK and free of defects.

_____ **4.** Install the wheel over the studs and start all lug nuts (or bolts) by hand.

_____ **5.** Tighten the lug nuts a little at a time in a star pattern using an air impact wrench equipped with the proper torque limiting adapter or a torque wrench.

_____ Used a torque wrench

_____ Used an air impact with a torque limiting adapter (torque stick)

_____ **6.** Tighten the lug nuts to final torque in a star pattern.

NOTE: "Tighten one, skip one, tighten one" is the usual method if four or five lug nuts are used.

49

Disc Brake Identification

Meets NATEF Task: None Specified

Name _____ Date _____ Time on Task _____

Make/Model _____ Year _____ Evaluation: 4   3   2   1

_____ **1.** Check service information and/or check the vehicle to determine the following
information:

        A. Type of brake system _____
             ___ Disc front brakes/drum rear brakes
             ___ Disc front brakes/disc rear brakes

        B. Type of disc brake caliper (check all that apply) _____

             ___ Floating
             ___ Sliding
             ___ Fixed
             ___ Single piston
             ___ Two pistons
             ___ Four or six pistons

        C. Type of rotors (check all that
           apply) _____

             ___ Vented front
             ___ Vented rear
             ___ Solid front
             ___ Solid rear

        D. Location of caliper (forward or rearward) _____

             Front calipers = _____
             Rear calipers = _____

        E. What sensor or switch is used to turn on the red brake warning light in the
           event of hydraulic failure?

             ___ Brake fluid level sensor
             ___ Pressure differential switch

50

Disc Brake Problem Diagnosis

Meets NATEF Task: (A5-D-1) Diagnose poor stopping noise, vibration, pulling, grabbing, dragging or pulsation concerns; determine necessary action (P-1)

Name _____ Date _____ Time on Task _____

Make/Model _____ Year _____ Evaluation: 4 3 2 1

_____ **1.** Verify disc brake problem concerns.

      _____ Noise (describe) _____

      _____ Poor stopping _____

      _____ Pulling (toward which side?) _____

      _____ Grabbing (when?) _____

      _____ Dragging _____

      _____ Brake pedal pulsation _____

_____ **2.** Hoist the vehicle safely. Wet the brake caliper or install a vacuum enclosure to provide protection against possible asbestos dust.

_____ **3.** Remove the caliper from the mounting and carefully inspect for leaks of the caliper, pads, mounts, and hardware.

      OK _____ **NOT OK** _____ Describe faults:

      _____

_____ **4.** Check rotor for excessive rust or damage. **OK** _____ **NOT OK** _____

_____ **5.** Measure the rotor and compare with factory specifications.

      OK _____ **NOT OK** _____

_____ **6.** Carefully inspect the caliper mounts for wear or damage.

_____ **7.** Based on the inspection, what is the necessary action?

      _____

51

Front Disc Brake Inspection

Meets NATEF Task: (A5-D-2) Remove caliper assembly, inspect for leaks and damage to caliper housing; determine necessary action. (P-1)

Name _____ Date _____ Time on Task _____

Make/Model _____ Year _____ Evaluation: 4 3 2 1

_____ 1. Hoist the vehicle safely and remove the front wheels.

_____ 2. Loosen the bleeder valve and push the caliper piston into the caliper.

_____ 3. Remove the caliper and pads.

_____ 4. Check the front disc pad condition (the thickness of the friction material should be thicker than the metal part of the pads), and the thickness should be equal on both sides of the rotor.

      OK ____   NOT OK ____   Describe any faults _____

_____ 5. Check the caliper mountings for damage or wear.

_____ 6. Check for brake fluid leaks and cracked flex hoses.

      OK ____   NOT OK ____

_____ 7. Based on the inspection results, what is the necessary action?

_____

_____

_____

_____

52

Caliper Mounting and Slide

Meets NATEF Task: (A5-D-3) Clean and inspect caliper mounting and slides/pins for operation, wear, and damage; determine necessary action. (P-1)

Name _____ Date _____ Time on Task _____

Make/Model _____ Year _____ Evaluation: 4 3 2 1

_____ **1.** Check service information for the specified cleaning and measurements for caliper slides and/or mounting points.

_____

_____

_____ **2.** Remove the calipers from the steering knuckle assembly and describe the type of mounting (check all that apply):

     ___ Sliding-type caliper
     ___ Guide pin-mounted caliper
     ___ Fixed caliper

_____ **3.** Inspect the mounting and slides for wear (describe):

        _____

        _____

        _____

        _____

        OK ____   NOT OK ____

_____ **4.** Based on the inspection and the vehicle manufacturer's recommended procedures, what is the necessary action?

_____

_____

53

Remove and Inspect Disc Brake Pads

Meets NATEF Task: (A5-D-4) Remove, inspect, and replace pads and retaining hardware; determine necessary action. (P-1)

Name _____ Date _____ Time on Task _____

Make/Model _____ Year _____ Evaluation: 4 3 2 1

_____ **1.** Check the service information for the specified procedure for removing and re installing disc brake pads. _____

_____

_____

_____ **2.** The procedure usually includes the following steps.

    A. Hoist the vehicle safely to a good working height.

    B. Remove the wheels.

    C. Remove the caliper retaining bolts and slide the caliper assembly off of the rotor.

> **NOTE:** The caliper piston may need to be pushed into the caliper to provide the necessary clearance to remove the caliper from the rotor. Most vehicle manufacturers recommend that the bleeder valve be opened before the caliper piston is pushed inward to prevent brake fluid from being forced backward into the ABS hydraulic unit or master cylinder.

    D. Remove the pads from the caliper and inspect them for wear, cracks, and chips.   **OK** _____   **NOT OK** _____

_____ **3.** Based on the inspection, what is the necessary action?

    _____

    _____

    _____

54

Disc Brake Caliper Overhaul

Meets NATEF Task: (A5-D-5) Disassemble and clean caliper assembly, inspect parts for wear, rust, scoring, and damage; replace seal, boot, and damaged or worn parts. (P-1)

Name _____ Date _____ Time on Task _____

Make/Model _____ Year _____ Evaluation: 4 3 2 1

_____ 1. Check the service information for the specified disc brake caliper overhaul procedure.

_____

_____ 2. Hoist the vehicle safely and remove the wheels.

_____ 3. Open the bleeder valve and compress the piston.

> **NOTE:** If the bleeder valve breaks or if the piston does not retract, consider replacing the caliper instead of overhauling it.

_____ 4. Remove the brake line and the caliper assembly from the vehicle.

> **NOTE:** Remove one caliper at a time to avoid the possible problem of installing the caliper on the wrong side of the vehicle.

_____ 5. Place a block of wood or a shop cloth beside the caliper piston and use compressed air to remove the piston, dust boot, and caliper O-ring.

_____ 6. Clean the caliper assembly and piston. _____**Piston OK** _____**Piston pitted**

_____ 7. Thoroughly coat the new square-cut O-ring and install it in the groove in the caliper housing.

_____ 8. Install the piston into the caliper.

_____ 9. Install the caliper using new disc brake pads as necessary and new copper washers on both sides of the banjo bolt, if equipped.

_____ 10. Bleed the caliper and repeat on the other side of the vehicle.

_____ 11. Depress the brake pedal to ensure a firm brake pedal and test for proper brake operation.

55

Disc Brake Caliper Assembly

Meets NATEF Task: (A5-D-6) Reassemble, lubricate and reinstall the calipers, pads, and related hardware, seat pads, and inspect for leaks. (P-1)

Name _____ Date _____ Time on Task _____

Make/Model _____ Year _____ Evaluation: 4 3 2 1

_____ **1.** Check the service information for the specified procedure to follow for reassembly of the caliper assembly. _____

_____

_____ **2.** The procedure usually includes the following steps.

    A. Thoroughly clean the caliper using denatured alcohol.

    B. Install new square-cut O-rings into the groove in the caliper bore and coat the bore and seal with clean brake fluid from a sealed container.

    C. Lubricate the caliper piston with clean brake fluid and install the caliper piston dust boot on the piston and then install the piston into the bore.

    D. Seat the caliper piston dust seal.

    E. Seat the pads as specified by the service information.

    _____

    _____

    _____

    F. Install the caliper on the vehicle.

_____ **3.** After installation of the caliper and pads, bleed the system.

_____ **4.** Check for leaks and proper operation.

56

Brake Pad Wear Indicator System (A5-D-13)

Meets NATEF Task: (A5-D-11) Check brake pad wear indicator system operation; determine necessary action. (P-2)

Name _____ Date _____ Time on Task _____

Make/Model _____ Year _____ Evaluation: 4 3 2 1

_____ 1. Check service information for the specified procedure to follow when checking the brake pad wear indicator system. Describe specified instructions: _____

_____

_____

_____ 2. What type of brake pad wear indicates that the system was tested? (check all that apply)

        _____ **Wear sensor on pads** (makes noise when pads are worn)

        _____ **Dash warning lamp** (triggered by the sensor in the brake)

        _____ **Slits cut in the disc brake pads** that indicate minimum allowable thickness

![Brake pads photo]

_____ 3. Based on the inspection of the brake pad wear indicator system, what is the necessary action?

_____

57

Disc Brake Pad Burnish/Break-In

Meets NATEF Task: (A5-D-12) Describe disc brake pad burnish/break-in procedure. (P-1)

Name _____ Date _____ Time on Task _____

Make/Model _____ Year _____ Evaluation: 4 3 2 1

_____ **1.** Check service information for the specified procedure for burnishing (breaking-in) new disc brake pads. Describe the specified procedure.

_____

_____

_____

_____

_____

_____ **2.** If a specified burnish procedure is not available, perform the following steps:

Step 1 – Make 6 to 10 brake applications from approximately 35 mph (56 km/h) with moderate brake pedal force.

Step 2 – Make an additional two to three hard brake applications from approximately 45 mph (72 km/h).

NOTE: Do not allow the vehicle to come to a complete stop. After performing these brake applications, allow the brakes to cool completely before driving again.

58

Rear Disc Parking Brake Adjustment

Meets NATEF Task: (A5-D-10) Retract caliper piston on an integrated parking brake system. (P-3)

Name _____ Date _____ Time on Task _____

Make/Model _____ Year _____ Evaluation: 4 3 2 1

Many vehicles equipped with rear disc brakes use a mechanical activated parking brake that is integral with the caliper. Most are designed to be self-adjusting by adjusting when excessive brake pad-to-rotor clearance occurs.

_____ **1.** Check the service information for the specified rear disc brake parking brake adjustment procedure.

_____

_____ **2.** Check the number of "clicks" of the parking brake.
_____ Number of clicks (should be between 3 and 9)

OK _____ **NOT OK** _____

If over 10 clicks is needed to set the parking brake, the rear disc brake caliper needs adjustment.

_____ **3.** Hoist the vehicle safely and remove both rear wheels.

_____ **4.** Carefully inspect the rear disc brakes for damage and measure the pads for excessive wear.

¼" DRILL
BIT OR DOWEL

OK _____ **NOT OK** _____

Replace the pads if worn to the minimum allowable thickness.

_____ **5.** If the disc brake pads are serviceable, operate the parking brake lever using the appropriate size wrench on the actuating arm retaining bolt/nut while lightly tapping on the caliper using a dead blow plastic hammer. The adjusting mechanism should cause the piston to be repositioned with the correct pad to rotor clearance.

OK _____ **NOT OK** _____

If the proper clearance is not achieved, replacement of the calipers is required.

59

Parking Brake Adjustment

Meets NATEF Task: (A5-F-3) Check parking brake cables and components for wear and clean, lubricate, adjust or replace as necessary (P-2)

Name _____ Date _____ Time on Task _____

Make/Model _____ Year _____ Evaluation: 4 3 2 1

_____ 1. Check the service information for the specified parking brake adjustment for the vehicle being serviced. _____

_____ 2. Apply the parking brake and count the number of "clicks."

       _____ less than 4 "clicks"
       _____ 5 - 10 "clicks"
       _____ over 10 "clicks"

    NOTE: If there are less than 4 "clicks" or more than 10 "clicks", adjustment of the parking brake may be necessary.

_____ 3. Place the gear selector in neutral and release the parking brake.

_____ 4. Hoist the vehicle safely.

_____ 5. Try rotating the rear wheels (front wheels on some Subaru vehicles).

       _____ rotates freely   _____ does not rotate

    NOTE: If the rear wheels do not rotate, try loosening the parking brake cable.

_____ 6. If the rear wheels rotate freely and the parking brake requires more than 10 "clicks," remove the rear brakes for inspection.

    NOTE: The parking brake should only be adjusted after checking and adjusting the rear brakes.

_____ 7. Clean and adjust the rear brakes.

_____ 8. Reassemble the rear brakes and apply the parking brake 3 - 4 "clicks."

_____ 9. If the rear wheels can be rotated, adjust the parking brake adjuster until the rear wheel brakes are just touching the brake drums.

_____ 10. Apply the parking brake and again count the "clicks." Most vehicle manufacturers recommend that the parking brake should hold with 6 to 18 "clicks." Readjust the parking brake as necessary.

60

Parking Brake Operation

Meets NATEF Task: (A5-F-4) Check parking brake and indicator light system operation; determine necessary action. (P-1)

Name _____ Date _____ Time on Task _____

Make/Model _____ Year _____ Evaluation: 4   3   2   1

_____ **1.** Check service information for the specified procedure to follow when checking the parking brake for proper operation.

_____

_____

_____

_____ **2.** Identify the type of parking brake.

_____ Foot operated

_____ Hand operated

_____ Push button

_____ **3.** Most vehicle manufacturers specify that the parking brake be applied and that the number of "clicks" required should be from 3 to 10. Apply the parking brake.

_____ **OK** (within the specified number of clicks)

_____ **NOT OK** (describe) _____

_____

_____ **4.** Based on the check of the parking brake, what is the necessary action?

_____

_____

61

Parking Brake Indicator Light

Meets NATEF Task: (A5-F-5) Check operation of brake stop light system; determine necessary action. (P-1)

Name _____ Date _____ Time on Task _____

Make/Model _____ Year _____ Evaluation: 4 3 2 1

A dash warning lamp should light whenever the parking brake is applied when the ignition is on. To verify that the parking brake indicator light functions correctly, follow these steps.

_____ 1. Turn the ignition to on (run).

> **NOTE:** The engine can be started to be sure that the ignition is on.

_____ 2. Apply the parking brake (check one of the following).

     ____ Hand-operated lever
     ____ Foot-operated pedal
     ____ Push button-operated parking brake

_____ 3. Did the red brake warning light come on?

     ____ Yes   ____ No

_____ 4. Check service information for the recommended procedures to follow if the parking brake indicator lamp did not work correctly.

_____

62

Brake Drum Measurement

Meets NATEF Task: (A5-C-2) Remove, clean, inspect, and measure brake drums; determine necessary action. (P-1)

Name _____ Date _____ Time on Task _____

Make/Model _____ Year _____ Evaluation: 4 3 2 1

_____ **1.** Wet the brake drum or use an enclosure to help protect against asbestos exposure.

_____ **2.** Remove the brake drum from the vehicle and label the left and right to ensure that the drum is replaced in the original location.

_____ **2.** Thoroughly inspect the brake drum.

- Hot (hard) spots

    OK_____ **NOT OK**_____ (requires replacement)

- Tap with a hammer. The brake drum should ring like a bell if not cracked.

    OK_____ **NOT OK**_____ (requires replacement)

_____ **3.** Determine the maximum allowable inside diameter of the brake drum or the maximum "turn to" dimension.

Maximum allowable inside diameter = _____ (allow 0.030" for wear)

Maximum "turn to" diameter = _____

_____ **4.** Measure the drum using a drum micrometer.

Left = _____   Right = _____

OK to machine _____   **NOT OK to machine** _____

_____ **5.** Based on the inspection, what is the necessary action? _____

_____

63

Machining a Brake Drum

Meets NATEF Task: (A5-C-3) Refinish brake drum; measure final drum diameter. (P-1)

Name _____ Date _____ Time on Task _____

Make/Model _____ Year _____ Evaluation: 4   3   2   1

_____ **1.** Measure the drum and double check that the brake drum can be safely machined.

- Maximum allowable inside diameter = _____
- Actual measurement of the drum = _____ left = _____ right = _____

OK to machine _____ **discard** _____

_____ **2.** Select the proper tapered centering cone and face supporting plate.

_____ **3.** Install a self-aligning spacer (SAS) and tighten the spindle nut.

_____ **4.** Perform a scratch cut.

_____ **5.** Stop the lathe, loosen the spindle nut, and rotate the brake drum 180° (one-half turn) and retighten the spindle nut.

_____ **6.** Perform a second scratch cut.

- If the second cut is in the same location, proceed with machining.
- If the second cut is on the opposite side of the drum, clean or repair the lathe before machining.

_____ **7.** Install a silencer band (vibration damper).

_____ **8.** Machine the drum.

_____ **9.** The measurement of the drum after machining = _____.

Does this allow 0.030" or more for wear?

Yes _____ (install on the vehicle)   **No** _____ (replace the drum)

64

Brake Rotor Measurement

Meets NATEF Task: (A5-D-6)Clean, inspect, and measure rotor thickness, lateral runout, and thickness variation; determine necessary action. (P-1)

Name _____ Date _____ Time on Task _____

Make/Model _____ Year _____ Evaluation: 4 3 2 1

_____ 1. Visually inspect the brake rotor for:

- hard spots **OK** ____ **NOT OK** ____ (requires replacement)

- excessive rust **OK** ____ **NOT OK** ____

- deep grooves (over 0.060" deep) **OK** ____ **NOT OK** ____

_____ 2. Check the service information and determine the specifications and measurements for thickness.

Minimum thickness = _____

Machine-to-thickness = _____

Actual thickness = _____ **OK** ____ **NOT OK** ____

_____ 3. Determine the specifications for thickness variation (parallelism).

_____

_____ 4. Using a micrometer, measure the thickness at four or more locations around the rotor to determine the thickness variation (parallelism). (Usually 0.0005" or less difference in the readings.)

A. _____   C. _____   E. _____

B. _____   D. _____   F. _____

OK ____   **NOT OK** ____

_____ 5. Use a dial indicator and measure the runout of the rotor.

Runout = _____ (should be less than 0.005 in.)

OK ____   **NOT OK** ____

_____ 6. Based on the measurements and manufacturer's recommendations, should the rotor be replaced or machined? Why? _____

_____

65

Remove and Replace a Disc Brake Rotor

Meets NATEF Task: (A5-D-7) Remove and reinstall rotor. (P-1)

Name _____ Date _____ Time on Task _____

Make/Model _____ Year _____ Evaluation: 4   3   2   1

_____ **1.** Hoist the vehicle safely and remove the wheels.

_____ **2.** Wet the disc brake caliper and pads or install a vacuum enclosure to provide protection against possible asbestos dust.

_____ **3.** Remove the caliper retaining fasteners and remove the caliper assembly.

_____ **4.** Use a stiff wire and support the caliper.

> **CAUTION:** Do not allow the caliper to hang by the flexible brake hose.

_____ **5.** Remove the disc brake rotor.

  A. If a hub-type rotor, remove the dust cover, cotter pins, retaining nut, and remove the bearings and rotor from the spindle.
  B. If a hubless rotor, remove the rotor from the hub.

_____ **6.** Clean the rotor contact surfaces.

_____ **7.** Reinstall the rotor. If a hub-type rotor, adjust the wheel bearing according to manufacturer's specifications.

_____ **8.** Reinstall the caliper assembly.

_____ **9.** Depress the brake pedal several times to restore proper braking action.

_____ **10.** Reinstall the wheels, torque the lug nuts to factory specifications, and lower the vehicle.

66

On-the-Vehicle Lathe

Meets NATEF Task: (A5-D-8) Refinish rotor on the vehicle; measure final rotor thickness.
(P-1)

Name _____ Date _____ Time on Task _____

Make/Model _____ Year _____ Evaluation: 4 3 2 1

_____ 1. Hoist the vehicle safely to the proper height according to the lathe manufacturer's instructions.

_____ 2. Mount the on-the-vehicle lathe according to the lathe manufacturer's instructions and calibrate the lathe as necessary.

> **NOTE:** On caliper mounted on-the-vehicle lathe, the disc brake caliper must be removed and supported with a wire to help prevent damage to the hydraulic flexible brake line.

_____ 3. Machine the rotor following the lathe manufacturer's instructions.

_____ 4. Use 150 grit aluminum oxide sandpaper on a block or a grinding disc to provide the required smooth non-directional finish.

_____ 5. Thoroughly clean both disc brake rotors before installing the replacement disc brake pads and reinstalling the disc brake caliper.

> **NOTE:** Be sure to install all anti-noise shims and hardware.

_____ 6. Reinstall the front wheels and tighten the lug nuts in a star pattern (tighten one, skip one, etc.) using a torque wrench on a torque-limiting adjuster with an air impact wrench.

_____ 7. Lower the vehicle and depress the brake pedal several times to achieve proper brake pedal height.

_____ 8. Test drive the vehicle before returning the vehicle to the customer.

67

We Support NATEF

Machining a Brake Rotor

Meets NATEF Task: (A5-D-9) Refinish rotor off the vehicle; measure final rotor thickness.
(P-1)

Name _____ Date _____ Time on Task _____

Make/Model _____ Year _____ Evaluation: 4   3   2   1

_____ 1. Carefully inspect the rotor for hot spots or damage.
            OK _____   **NOT OK** _____ (requires replacement of the rotor)

_____ 2. Determine minimum rotor thickness = _____ or machine to thickness = _____

_____ 3. Measure the rotor thickness = _____.
            OK to machine___   NOT OK to machine___

_____ 4. Clean the brake lathe spindle.

_____ 5. Select the proper tapered cover and/or collets to properly
       secure the rotor to the lathe spindle.

_____ 6. Install the self-aligning spacer (SAS) and
       tighten the spindle nut.

_____ 7. Install the silencer band (noise damper).

_____ 8. Perform a scratch test.

_____ 9. Stop the lathe and loosen the spindle nut.

_____ 10. Rotate the rotor 180° (one-half turn) and tighten the spindle nut.

_____ 11. Perform another scratch cut. If the second scratch cut is in the same location as the
first scratch cut or extends completely around the rotor, the machining of the rotor can
continue. (If the second scratch cut is 180 from the first scratch cut, remove the rotor
and clean the spindle and attaching hardware. Repeat the scratch test.)

_____ 12. Machine the rotor removing as little material as possible.

_____ 13. Measure the rotor with a micrometer to be sure rotor thickness is still within limits.

_____ 14. Use 150 grit aluminum oxide sandpaper on a block of wood for 60 seconds on each
side or a grinder to provide a smooth nondirectional finish.

_____ 15. Thoroughly clean the rotor friction surface.

_____ 16. Remove the rotor from the lathe.

68

Vacuum Power Brake Booster Test

Meets NATEF Task: (A5-E-1) Test pedal free travel; check power assist operation.
(P-2)

Name _____   Date _____   Time on Task _____

Make/Model _____   Year _____   Evaluation: 4   3   2   1

_____ **1.** Check the service information for the specified procedure for testing a vacuum power
brake booster for the vehicle being serviced.

_____

_____ **2.** With the engine off, depress the brake pedal several times until the brake pedal feels
hard (firm).

_____ **3.** The brake pedal should not fall to the floor of the vehicle.

OK _____   NOT OK _____

NOTE: If the brake pedal travels to the floor
of the vehicle, carefully inspect the hydraulic
brake system for a fault. Service or repair the
hydraulic brake problem before continuing
with this test.

_____ **4.** With your foot still firmly depressing the brake
pedal, start the engine. The brake pedal should
go down.

OK _____   NOT OK _____

_____ **5.** If the brake pedal did not go down when the engine was started, visually check the
following:

_____ Minimum of 15 in. Hg of vacuum to the vacuum booster from the engine
manifold or auxiliary vacuum pump

_____ Proper operation of the one-way check valve

_____ Unrestricted charcoal filter between the booster and the intake manifold (if
equipped)

_____ Inspect for vacuum leaks

OK _____   NOT OK _____

69

Vacuum Supply/Manifold or Auxiliary Pump

Meets NATEF Task: (A5-E-2) Check vacuum supply to vacuum-type power booster.
(P-1)

Name _____ Date _____ Time on Task _____

Make/Model _____ Year _____ Evaluation: 4 3 2 1

_____ 1. Check service information for the recommended procedures and specifications for checking vacuum supply to power booster.

_____

_____

_____

_____ 2. Is the vehicle equipped with an auxiliary vacuum pump?   ____ Yes ____ No

_____ 3. Most vehicle manufacturers specify that a vacuum "T" be installed in the vacuum line between the intake manifold and/or auxiliary pump and the vacuum power brake booster assembly. Most manufacturers specify a minimum of 15 in. Hg. of vacuum be measured.

Actual vacuum measured at the power brake booster = _____

____ OK ____ NOT OK

70

Vacuum-Type Power Booster

Meets NATEF Task: (A5-E-3) Inspect vacuum-type power booster unit for vacuum leaks; inspect the check valve for proper operation; determine necessary action. (P-1)

Name _____ Date _____ Time on Task _____

Make/Model _____ Year _____ Evaluation: 4 3 2 1

_____ 1. Check service information for the recommended procedures to follow to determine if a vacuum-type power brake booster has a vacuum leak.

_____

_____

_____

_____ 2. Most vacuum-type power boosters should be capable of supplying 3 or more assisted stops with the engine off. How many were found? _____

_____ 3. Most vehicle manufacturers specify checking for leaks both around the outside (under the hood), as well as in the valve area under the dash.

Under hood:

____ OK ____ NOT OK

Valve area:

____ OK ____ NOT OK

_____ 4. Based on the test results, what is the necessary action? _____

_____

71

Hydro-Boost Test

Meets NATEF Task: (A5-E-4) Inspect and test hydro-boost system for leaks and proper operation. (P-3)

Name _____ Date _____ Time on Task _____

Make/Model _____ Year _____ Evaluation: 4 3 2 1

_____ 1. Check the service information for the specified Hydro-Boost testing procedure for the vehicle being serviced.

_____

_____ 2. Start the testing of a Hydro-boost power brake assist system by carefully inspecting the following components:

Power steering fluid level	OK _____	NOT OK _____
Power steering pressure hoses for leaks	OK _____	NOT OK _____
Power steering pump drive belt	OK _____	NOT OK _____
Master cylinder brake fluid level	OK _____	NOT OK _____
Visually inspect the Hydro-boost assembly for evidence of power steering fluid leaks	OK _____	NOT OK _____

_____ 3. Check the operation of the base hydraulic brakes by depressing the brake pedal several times with the engine "off" until the brake pedal feels firm. Continue to apply force to the brake pedal. The brake pedal should *not* drop.
   OK _____ NOT OK _____ (master cylinder or hydraulic system fault is indicated)

_____ 4. With your foot still applying force to the brake pedal, start the engine. If the Hydro-boost system is functioning correctly, the brake pedal should drop.
   OK _____ NOT OK _____

_____ 5. To check the power steering pump for proper operation, connect a power steering pressure gauge or pressure and volume gauge between the pump and the Hydro-boost unit. Start the engine and observe the pressure and volume gauges.
   Pressure at idle = _____
   (should be less than 150 psi)
       OK _____ NOT OK _____

   Volume at idle = _____
   (should be at least 2 gallons per minute)
       OK _____ NOT OK _____

72

Master Cylinder Pushrod Length

Meets NATEF Task: (A5-E-5) Measure and adjust master cylinder pushrod length.
(P-3)

Name _____ Date _____ Time on Task _____

Make/Model _____ Year _____ Evaluation: 4 3 2 1

_____ **1.** Check service information for the specified procedures and specifications for checking
and adjusting master cylinder pushrod length.

_____

_____

VACUUM BRAKE
BOOSTER

ADJUSTER

VACUUM
HOSE

PUSHROD (HOLD)

_____ **2.** Where is the measurement taken?

_____

_____ **3.** Is a "go-no go" gauge needed? If so, what is the part number? _____

_____ **4.** Describe the symptoms if the master cylinder pushrod length is not correct.

_____

_____

73

Traction Control Identification

Meets NATEF Task: (A5-G-9) Identify traction/vehicle stability control system components.
(P-3)

Name _____ Date _____ Time on Task _____

Make/Model _____ Year _____ Evaluation: 4 3 2 1

_____ **1.** Check service information for what type and components are used in the traction
control/vehicle stability control system (check all that apply).

    ___ A. Rear-wheel only antilock braking system
    ___ B. A four-wheel (three channel, three wheel speed sensors) ABS
    ___ C. Four-wheel (four channel, four wheel speed sensors) ABS
    ___ D. Electronic throttle control (ETC) system
    ___ E. Electronic stability control dash-mounted switch
    ___ F. Electric power steering system (EPS)

_____ **2.** Describe the location of the following components:

    Antilock braking system hydraulic control unit _____

    Antilock braking system electronic control unit _____

    Wheel speed sensors _____

    Stability control system dash switch (if equipped) _____

74

ABS Component Inspection

Meets NATEF Task: (A5-G-1) Identify and inspect electronic brake control system components; determine needed action. (P-3)

Name _____ Date _____ Time on Task _____

Make/Model _____ Year _____ Evaluation: 4 3 2 1

_____ **1.** Check the brake fluid level and condition in the master cylinder.

       OK _____   **NOT OK** _____

       Describe _____

       _____

_____ **2.** Check the brake fluid level and condition in the ABS reservoir if equipped.

       _____ Not equipped with an ABS brake fluid reservoir

       OK _____   **NOT OK** _____ **Describe** _____

_____ **3.** Visually check the hydraulic control unit and accumulator for leakage or physical damage.

       OK _____   **NOT OK** _____ **Describe** _____

_____ **4.** Visually check all wheel speed sensors and tone wheel for damage or debris.

       OK _____   **NOT OK** _____ **Describe** _____

_____ **5.** Visually inspect the wheel speed sensor wiring harness for damage.

       OK _____   **NOT OK** _____ **Describe** _____

_____ **6.** Visually inspect the ABS controller for damage or corroded connection(s).

       OK _____   **NOT OK** _____ **Describe** _____

_____ **7.** Based on the inspection, what is the necessary action? _____

75

ABS Component Identification

Meets NATEF Task: (A5-G-1) Identify antilock system components; determine necessary action. (P-3)

Name _____ Date _____ Time on Task _____

Make/Model _____ Year _____ Evaluation: 4 3 2 1

_____ **1.** Type and/or brand of antilock system _____

_____ **2.** List the number and locations of the wheel speed sensors.   Number = _____

Locations (describe) _____

_____ **3.** Check the number of channels:

One (rear-wheel only) _____   Four channels   _____

Three channels   _____   Unknown   _____

_____ **4.** How many accumulators?

_____ zero   _____ one   _____ two

_____ other (describe) _____

_____ **5.** Describe the bleeding procedure (see service information): _____

_____

_____

_____ **6.** Describe the diagnostic trouble code retrieval method: _____

_____

_____

_____ **7.** What are the wheel speed sensor specifications? (See service information.)

Front = _____   Adjustable? _____ Specs. _____

Rear = _____   Adjustable? _____ Specs. _____

_____ **8.** Equipped with traction control? **Yes** _____   **No** _____

_____ **9.** List the stored diagnostic trouble codes (DTCs): _____

_____

_____ **10.** Based on the diagnosis, what is the necessary action? _____

_____

76

Diagnose ABS System Concerns

Meets NATEF Task: (A5-G-4) Diagnose ABS operational concerns; determine necessary action. (P-2)

Name _____ Date _____ Time on Task _____

Make/Model _____ Year _____ Evaluation: 4 3 2 1

_____ **1. Poor stopping** – Check the following system or components.

    A. Tires – condition and sizes   OK _____   NOT OK _____

    B. Base brake components such as calipers, pads, and drive brake components

         OK _____   NOT OK _____

_____ **2. Abnormal pedal feel or pulsation** – Check the following components.

    A. Wheel speed sensor tone ring or wiring for damage.

         OK _____   NOT OK _____

    B. Brake rotors and drum for out-of-round or other faults

         OK _____   NOT OK _____

    C. Master cylinder and brake fluid for level or contaminants

         OK _____   NOT OK _____

_____ **3. Wheel lockup** – Check the following components.

    A. Base brake friction material (pads and linings) for grease, excessive wear or contamination.

         OK _____   NOT OK _____

    B. Wheel speed sensor tone ring for damage

         OK _____   NOT OK _____

    C. Excessively worn or mismatched tires

         OK _____   NOT OK _____

_____ **4. Abnormal noise** – Check the following components.

    A. Accumulator leakage creating the need for extended pump operation

         OK _____   NOT OK _____

    B. Base brakes for excessive wear or defective friction components

         OK _____   NOT OK _____

_____ **5.** Based on the diagnosis, what is the necessary action? _____

77

ABS Code Retrieval and Erase

Meets NATEF Task: (A5-G-5) Diagnose ABS electronic control and component using self diagnosis; determine necessary action. (P-2)

Name _____ **Date** _____ **Time on Task** _____

Make/Model _____ **Year** _____ **Evaluation:** 4 3 2 1

The purpose of this worksheet is to become familiar with how to retrieve diagnostic trouble codes (DTCs) and how to correctly erase stored DTCs.

_____ 1. Identify the brand of ABS system by using the service information.

ABS (brand) = _____

_____ 2. Describe the specified method to retrieve an ABS diagnostic trouble code (DTC):

_____

_____

_____ 3. Set a code by disconnecting a relay or other easily reached component.

Component unplugged is _____

_____ 4. Did a diagnostic trouble code set?

Yes _____ No _____

_____ 5. Retrieve the code. What code set? _____

_____ 6. Did more than one code set?

Yes _____ No _____

_____ 7. Reconnect the relay or component.

_____ 8. Describe the specified method to use to clear a stored diagnostic trouble code:

_____

_____

_____ 9. Based on the diagnosis, what is the necessary action? _____

78

ABS Set a Code/Retrieve a Code

Meets NATEF Task: (A5-G-5) Diagnose ABS electronic control and components using recommended test equipment; determine necessary action. (P-2)

Name _____ Date _____ Time on Task _____

Make/Model _____ Year _____ Evaluation: 4 3 2 1

The purpose of this worksheet is to become familiar with how an ABS diagnostic trouble code (DTC) is set and how to retrieve the code.

_____ **1.** Disconnect a wheel speed sensor at the connector or electro-hydraulic unit.

_____ **2.** Start the engine (or drive the vehicle) until the amber ABS malfunction indicator lamp on the dash comes on.

_____ **3.** What method was used to retrieve the DTC?

           _____ scan tool

           _____ flash code ("key" or jumper wire)

           _____ other (describe) _____

_____ **4.** What DTCs were set?

        DTC # _____ What is the meaning of this code? _____

        DTC # _____ What is the meaning of this code? _____

_____ **5.** Reconnect the wheel speed sensor or electro-mechanical electrical connector.

_____ **6.** What method is recommended to clear the DTCs? _____

_____

_____ **7.** Retest the vehicle checking for proper brake and ABS operation.

_____ **8.** Based on the diagnosis, what is the necessary action? _____

_____

79

Depressurization of High-Pressure ABS

Meets NATEF Task: (A5-G-6) Depressurize high-pressure components of the electronic brake control system. (P-3)

Name _____ Date _____ Time on Task _____

Make/Model _____ Year _____ Evaluation: 4 3 2 1

Integral ABS systems combine the function of the master cylinder, power-assist booster, and antilock brake functions in one assembly. These assemblies operate at high pressure and must be depressurized before performing service work on the brake system to avoid possible personal injury.

_____ 1. Check the service information for the specified depressurization procedure for the vehicle being serviced.

_____

_____

_____ 2. Visually check the brake fluid reservoir.

Proper level?   OK _____   NOT OK _____

Brake fluid condition? Describe: _____

_____ 3. Inspect the ABS hydraulic control unit for signs of damage or leakage.

OK _____   NOT OK _____

_____ 4. With the ignition key off, depress the brake pedal forty (40) times. The brake pedal should be hard when depressed after the first few brake applications

OK _____   NOT OK _____

If the brake pedal is not hard and a power-assisted brake application is still possible, find and correct the ignition feed circuit to the hydraulic control unit before proceeding to brake system service.

80

Bleed ABS Hydraulic Circuits

Meets NATEF Task: (A5-G-7) Bleed electronic brake control system hydraulic circuits. (P-1)

Name _____ Date _____ Time on Task _____

Make/Model _____ Year _____ Evaluation: 4 3 2 1

ABS hydraulic front and rear hydraulic circuits must be bled using the exact procedure specified by the vehicle manufacturer.

_____ 1. Check the service information and state the vehicle manufacturer's specified bleeding procedure and sequence.

_____

_____

_____

_____

_____ 2. Type of brake fluid specified for use during the bleeding procedure?

_____

_____ 3. Was a scan tool required? ____ Yes ____ No If yes, describe the procedure:

_____

_____ 4. Was a special tool or tools required? ____ Yes ____ No If yes, describe the procedure:

_____

_____ 5. Was the bleeding procedure the same for both the front and the rear wheel brakes?

____ Yes ____ No

81

Remove and Install ABS Components

Meets NATEF Task: (None Specified)

Name _____ Date _____ Time on Task _____

Make/Model _____ Year _____ Evaluation: 4 3 2 1

_____ **1.** Describe an ABS fault that requires the replacement of the ABS component if applicable.

_____

_____

_____

_____ **2.** State the vehicle manufacturer's specified removal and reinstallation procedure.

_____

_____

_____

_____ **3.** What unit/component is to be removed?

_____

        Instructors OK _____

_____ **4.** List the cautions and warnings that were included in the service procedure.

_____

_____

_____ **5.** Time needed to perform this operation? _____

_____ **6.** Describe any problems encountered during this procedure.

_____

_____

82

ABS Wheel Speed Sensor Testing

Meets NATEF Task: (A5-G-8) Test, diagnose, and service ABS wheel speed sensors. (P-3)

Name _____ **Date** _____ **Time on Task** _____

Make/Model _____ **Year** _____ **Evaluation:** 4 3 2 1

A magnetic wheel speed sensor can fail in a variety of ways including: electrically shorted, open, or grounded.

_____ **1.** Locate and disconnect the wheel speed sensor connector. Hoist the vehicle if necessary.

_____ **2.** Disconnect the wheel speed sensor (WSS) connector and connect a digital meter set to read ohms.

_____ **3.** Measure the resistance at the sensor terminals.

        WSS resistance = _____

        Compare the resistance to the factory
        specifications = _____
        (usually about 1000 ohms).
        OK _____   **NOT OK** _____

_____ **4.** With the meter still set to read ohms, connect one meter lead to a good clean chassis ground and the other lead to one terminal of the WSS connector. This test determines that the WSS is shorted to ground unless the meter indicates infinity (OL).

        Meter reading = _____ should be infinity (OL). **OK** _____   **NOT OK** _____

_____ **5.** Set the digital meter to read AC volts.

_____ **6.** Connect the leads of the meter to the terminals of the wheel speed sensor.

_____ **7.** Have an assistant spin the wheel and observe the AC voltage on the meter display.

        Reading = _____ AC volts (should be over 0.1 V (100 mV)

        OK _____   **NOT OK** _____

_____ **8.** Observe the wheel speed sensor using a graphing multimeter (GMM) or a digital storage oscilloscope (DSO). Draw the waveform displayed while an assistant spins the wheel.

83

Modified Vehicle ABS Problem Diagnosis

Meets NATEF Task: (A5-G-9) Diagnose electronic brake control system braking concerns caused by vehicle modifications (tire size, curb height, final drive ratio, etc.). (P-3)

Name _____ Date _____ Time on Task _____

Make/Model _____ Year _____ Evaluation: 4 3 2 1

_____ **1.** Carefully inspect the vehicle for modifications such as changes made to wheels/tires, axle ratio, and curb height.

Tire size: **OK** _____ **NOT OK** _____ (describe) _____

Curb (ride) height: ___ stock ___ higher ___ lower (describe) _____

Axle ratio: ___ stock ___ unknown (describe) _____

_____ **2.** Be sure that all four tires are the same size and brand.

LF tire size = _____ Brand = _____

RF tire size = _____ Brand = _____

RR tire size = _____ Brand = _____

LR tire size = _____ Brand = _____

_____ **3.** Did any of the modifications affect the braking?

___ **Yes**

___ **No** (describe) _____

_____ **4.** Did the modifications set an ABS diagnostic trouble code (DTC)?

___ **Yes** (describe) _____

___ **No**

_____ **5.** Check the service information and record the specified procedure to follow when servicing an antilock brake system on a vehicle that has been modified.

_____

84

Traction Control/Vehicle Stability ID

Meets NATEF Task: (A5-G-2) Identify traction control/vehicle stability control system components. (P-3)

Name _____ Date _____ Time on Task _____

Make/Model _____ Year _____ Evaluation: 4 3 2 1

_____ **1.** Check service information to determine what components are included in the traction control/vehicle stability control system (check all that apply).

        ___ ABS electrohydraulic control unit
        ___ ABS/traction control computer (controller)
        ___ Wheel speed sensors
        ___ Steering wheel position sensor
        ___ Vehicle speed sensor
        ___ Lateral force ("G") sensor

![Photograph of an ABS/traction control module labeled WKH1 mounted in a vehicle]

_____ **2.** Describe the location of each of the components.

_____

_____

_____

_____

_____

85

Regenerative Braking System Identification

Meets NATEF Task: (A5-G-3) Describe the operation of a regenerative braking system. (P-3)

Name _____ Date _____ Time on Task _____

Make/Model _____ Year _____ Evaluation: 4 3 2 1

Regenerative braking systems are found on hybrid electric vehicles (HEV). Check service information for the description of operation, components, and component locations.

_____ **1.** Regenerative braking system operation (as per service information):

_____

_____

_____ **2.** What is the location of the electrohydraulic control system?

_____

_____

_____

_____

_____

_____ **3.** Describe the master cylinder and associated components:

_____

_____

_____ **4.** Describe the base brake system:

_____

_____ **5.** What specific service procedures for the base brakes are needed because of the regenerative braking system?

_____

_____

APPENDIX

BRAKES, 7th

STUDENT CHECK OFF SHEETS

James D. Halderman

Task Sheet Name	Task Sheet Page	Date Completed	Instructor OK
Chapter 1 - Service Information, Tools, and Safety			
Safety Check (None Specified)	1		
Vehicle Hoisting (None Specified)	2		
Fire Extinguisher (None Specified)	3		
Work Order (A5-A-1)	4		
Vehicle Brake System Information (A5-A-3)	5		
Base Brake Identification (A5-A-3)	6		
VIN Code (A5-A-4)	7		
Chapter 2 - Environmental and Hazardous Materials			
Material Safety Data Sheet (None Specified)	8		
Chapter 3 – Braking System Components and Performance Standards			
Identify and Interpret Brake Concerns (A5-A-2)	9		
Brake System Component ID (None Specified)	10		
Chapter 4 – Braking System Principles and Friction Materials			
Brake System Principles (None Specified)	11		
Brake Performance Identification (None Specified)	12		
Chapter 5 – Brake Hydraulic Systems			
Hydraulic Pressure Analysis (A5-B-1)	13		
Brake Pedal Height (A5-B-2)	14		
Master Cylinder Operation Testing (A5-B-3)	15		
Bench Bleeding the Master Cylinder (A5-B-4)	16		
Hydraulic System Fault Analysis (A5-B-5)	17		
Chapter 6 – Hydraulic Valves and Switches			
Metering Valve Inspection and Testing (A5-B-10)	18		
Proportioning Valve Inspection and Testing (A5-B-10)	19		
Pressure Differential Switch Inspection (A5-B-10)	20		
Height-Sensing Proportioning Valves (A5-B-10)	21		
Red Brake Warning Lamp Diagnosis (A5-B-11)	22		
Brake Stop Light Switch (A5-F-6)	23		
Chapter 7 – Brake Fluid and Lines			
Brake Hose and Line Inspection (A5-B-6)	24		
Brake Line and Hose Replacement (A5-B-7)	25		
Brake Line Flaring (A5-B-8)	26		
Brake Fluid (A5-B-9)	27		
Brake Fluid Contamination Test (A5-B-13	28		

Task Sheet Name	Task Sheet Page	Date Completed	Instructor OK
Chapter 8 – Brake Bleeding Methods and Procedures			
Manual Brake Bleeding (A5-B-12)	29		
Pressure Brake Bleeding (A5-B-12)	30		
Vacuum Brake Bleeding (A5-B-12)	31		
Gravity Brake Bleeding (A5-B-12)	32		
Surge Brake Bleeding (A5-B-12)	33		
Brake Fluid Flush and Fill (A5-B-12)	34		
Chapter 9 – Wheel Bearings and Service			
Wheel Bearing Diagnosis (A5-F-1)	35		
Wheel Bearing Service (A5-F-2)	36		
Wheel Bearing and Race Replacement (A5-F-6)	37		
Inspect and Replace Wheel Studs (A5-F-8)	38		
Sealed Wheel Bearing Replacement (A5-F-7)	39		
Chapter 10 – Drum Brakes			
Drum Brake Identification (None Specified)	40		
Chapter 11 – Drum Brake Diagnosis and Service			
Drum Brake Problem Diagnosis (A5-C-1)	41		
Drum Brake Inspection (A5-C-4)	42		
Drum Brake Overhaul (A5-C-4)	43		
Dual Servo Drum Brake (A5-C-4)	44		
Leading/Trailing Drum Brake (A5-C-4)	45		
Wheel Cylinder Inspection and Replacement (A5-C-5)	46		
Pre-Adjustment of Brake Shoes (A5-C-6)	47		
Install Wheel and Torque Lug Nuts (A5-A-4)	48		
Chapter 12 – Disc Brakes			
Disc Brake Identification (None Specified)	49		
Chapter 13 – Disc Brake Diagnosis and Service			
Disc Brake Problem Diagnosis (A5-D-1)	50		
Front Disc Brake Inspection (A5-D-2)	51		
Caliper Mounting and Slide (A5-D-3)	52		
Remove and Inspect Disc Brake Pads (A5-D-4)	53		
Disc Brake Caliper Overhaul (A5-D-5)	54		
Disc Brake Caliper Assembly (A5-D-6)	55		
Brake Pad Wear Indicator System (A5-D-11)	56		
Brake Pad Burnish/Break-In (A5-D-12)	57		

Task Sheet Name	Task Sheet Page	Date Completed	Instructor OK
Chapter 14 – Parking Brake Operation, Diagnosis, and Service			
Rear Disc Parking Brake Adjustment (A5-D-10)	58		
Parking Brake Adjustment (A5-F-3)	59		
Parking Brake Operation (A5-F-5)	60		
Parking Brake Indicator Light (A5-F-5)	61		
Chapter 15 – Machining Brake Drums and Rotors			
Brake Drum Measurement (A5-C-2)	62		
Machining a Brake Drum (A5-C-3)	63		
Brake Rotor Measurement (A5-D-6)	64		
Remove and Replace a Disc Brake Rotor (A5-D-7)	65		
On-the-Vehicle Lathe (A5-D-8)	66		
Machining a Brake Rotor (A5-D-9)	67		
Chapter 16 – Power Brake Unit Operation, Diagnosis, and Service			
Vacuum Power Brake Booster Test (A5-E-1)	68		
Vacuum Supply/Manifold or Auxiliary Pump (A5-E-2)	69		
Vacuum-Type Power Booster Unit (A5-E-3)	70		
Hydro-Boost Test (A5-E-4)	71		
Master Cylinder Pushrod Length (A5-E-5)	72		
Chapter 17 – ABS Components and Operation			
Traction Control Identification (A5-G-9)	73		
Chapter 18 – ABS Diagnosis and Service			
ABS Component Inspection (A5-G-1)	74		
ABS Component Identification (A5-G-1)	75		
Diagnose ABS System Concerns (A5-G-4)	76		
ABS Code Retrieval and Erase (A5-G-5)	77		
ABS Set a Code/Retrieve a Code (A5-G-5)	78		
Depressurization of High-Pressure ABS (A5-G-6)	79		
Bleed ABS Hydraulic Circuits (A5-G-7)	80		
Remove and Install ABS Components (None Specified)	81		
ABS Wheel Speed Sensor Testing (A5-G-8)	82		
Modified Vehicle ABS Problem Diagnosis (A5-G-9)	83		
Chapter 19 – Electronic Stability Control System			
Traction Control/Vehicle Stability Component Identification (A5-G-2)	84		
Chapter 20 – Regenerative Braking Systems			
Regenerative Braking System ID (A5-G-3)	85